Virginia Woolf's Nose

Hermione Lee

Virginia Woolf's Nose

Essays
on Biography

PRINCETON UNIVERSITY PRESS

PRINCETON AND OXFORD

Copyright © 2005 by Hermione Lee

Requests for permission to reproduce material from this work should be sent to Permissions, Princeton University Press

Published by Princeton University Press, 41 William Street, Princeton, New Jersey 08540

In the United Kingdom: Princeton University Press, 3 Market Place, Woodstock, Oxfordshire OX20 1SY

Library of Congress Cataloging-in-Publication Data

Lee, Hermione.
 Virginia Woolf's nose: essays on biography / Hermione Lee.
 p. cm.
 Includes bibliographical references and index.
 Contents: Shelley's heart and Pepys's lobsters—Virginia Woolf's nose—Jane Austen faints—How to end it all.
 ISBN 0-691-12032-3 (acid-free paper)
 1. Authors, English—Biography—History and criticism. 2. Biography as a literary form. 3. Shelley, Percy Bysshe, 1792–1822. 4. Woolf, Virginia, 1882–1941. 5. Pepys, Samuel, 1633–1703. 6. Austen, Jane, 1775–1817. I. Title.

PR106.L44 2005
820.9'492—dc22   2004058457

British Library Cataloging-in-Publication Data is available

This book has been composed in Janson with American Typewriter Display

Printed on acid-free paper. ∞

pup.princeton.edu

Printed in the United States of America

10 9 8 7 6 5 4 3 2 1

Contents

Acknowledgments

I should like to thank the following: Ian Donaldson and Richard Holmes for inviting me to the Cambridge Seminar on "Biographical Knowledge" where I tried out some of these ideas; Princeton University Press for inviting me to give the J. Edward Farnum Lectures which make up the first three chapters of this book; my agent Pat Kavanagh; my husband John Barnard; my students in the biography seminars at Oxford over the last five years; Dinah Birch, Lucy Newlyn, Hugh Haughton, and Roy Foster for conversations about life-writing; and Jenny Uglow, for inspiration and friendship. I am grateful to all at Princeton University Press who have worked on this book and to my friends at Princeton (including Michael Wood, Christine Stansell, Deborah Nord, and Paul Muldoon) for hospitality and encouragement. The final stages of the work on this book were done at the Dorothy and Lewis B. Cullman Center for Scholars and Writers at the New York Public Library, as a Mel and Lois Tukman Fellow from 2004–2005.

The author and publisher are grateful to Julian Barnes, Michael Cunningham, and Mark Doty for permission to quote their words, and to Faber & Faber, Ltd., for permission to quote some lines from Philip Larkin's "Aubade."

Virginia Woolf's Nose

....

Introduction

We all want stories. As readers of biography, we are like the audience Elizabeth Gaskell was thinking of when she noted to herself, as she started her life of Charlotte Brontë, "Get as many anecdotes as possible. If you love your reader and want to be read, get anecdotes!"[1] The trouble with death, Henry James thought, is that it "smooths the folds" of the person one loved. "The figure retained by the memory is compressed and intensified; accidents have dropped away from it and shades have ceased to count; it stands, sharply, for a few estimated and cherished things, rather than nebulously, for a swarm of possibilities."[2] The critic David Ellis cites this profound passage as a way into talking about the problems of biography: that it can tend to sound too knowing and firm about the shape of its subject's life, to make it read too smoothly, to be too selective. Alternatives, missed chances, roads not taken, accidents and hesitations, the whole "swarm of possibilities" that hums around our every experience, too often disappears in the smoothing biographical process.

Whether we think of biography as more like history or more like fiction, what we want from it is a vivid sense of the person. The reader's first question of the biographer is always going to be, what was she, or he, like? Other questions (like why, or how do you know, or do we approve, or does it matter?) may follow. But "likeness" must be there. And when we are reading other forms of life-writing—autobiography, memoir, journal, letter, autobiographical fiction, or poem—or when we are trying ourselves to tell the story of a life, whether in an obituary, or in a conversation, or in a confession, or in a book, we are always drawn to moments of intimacy, revelation, or particular inwardness.

Readers of biography are greedy readers, with an insatiable appetite for detail and story. There are all kinds of ways of satisfying these appetites. Coming at a likeness will always involve a messy, often contradictory, mixture of approaches. It's that all-encompassing quality which gives biography some of its appeal—and makes it so resistant to theorising. History, politics, sociology, gossip, fiction, literary criticism, psychoanalysis, documentary, journalism, ethics, and philosophy are all scrambled up inside the genre. But the target of all these approaches is a living person in a body, not a smoothed-over figure. What makes biography so endlessly absorbing is that through all the documents and letters and witnesses, the conflicting opinions and partial memories and fictionalised versions, we keep catching sight of a real body, a physical life: the young Dickens coming quickly into a room, sprightly, long-haired, bright-eyed, dandyish, in a crimson velvet waistcoat or tartan trousers; the sound of Coleridge's voice as he talked magically on and on; Rimbaud, dust-covered and scrawny and dressed in baggy grey khaki trousers, leading a caravan of camels across the desert sands of Abyssinia; Joyce with a black felt hat, thick glasses and a cigar, sitting in Sylvia Beach's bookshop in Paris; Edith Wharton and Henry James, veiled and hatted, tucked up comfortably in the back of the Panhard behind the chauffeur, exchanging impressions as they zoom along the empty French roads.

Biography has changed enormously in the last hundred years in what it allows itself to talk about. Samuel Johnson and Thomas Carlyle, great British pioneers of life-writing, called above all for "veracity" rather than "panegyric," for a warts-and-all picture which should include the representation of "the minute details of daily life."[3] A more protective practice of idealising or censoring biography developed (though not exclusively) in the Victorian period. But with the increasing dominance, popularity, professionalisation, and—it must be added— scandal-mongering of biography in the twentieth century, real warts are now allowed to be included. The life of the body plays much more of a part in contemporary biographical narratives. Masturbation, dental work, body odour, menstruation, gonorrhea, addictions, and sexual preferences are all permissible subjects. As Virginia Woolf observes, "opinions change as the times change", and one of the biographer's jobs is to detect "the presence of obsolete conventions."[4] The comparison of death-bed scenes in biography which ends this book suggests how much conventions have shifted. But from the time that Dryden, writing in the 1680s, praised Plutarch's lives for showing us the domestic lives of great heroes like Alexander in their "private lodgings" and their "undress" ("the pageantry of life is taken away; you see the poor reasonable animal, as naked as nature ever made him; are made acquainted with his passions and his follies, and find the Demi-God a Man"),[5] biography has always directed us to the figure of a real person in all his or her peculiarity, accidentalness, and actuality.

But that imitation of reality may be put together out of all kinds of bits and pieces, contradictions, myths and mysteries. *Virginia Woolf's Nose* presents a variety of case-studies where the biographer is faced with gaps and absences and unprovable stories. The aim is to ask, by looking in detail at such examples, how a life can be brought home to us. How do biographers deal with moments of physical shock, with the subject's secret bodily life, with the mystery of death, and with the aftermath of rumour and reputation? How do they nose out the personality and the life of the writer through the often ambiguous or deceptive evidence of their work? What part do blame, resentment, personal affection, idealisation, judgment, and defensiveness have to play in the courtroom drama of life-writing? Where do biographers start from, and how do they know when to stop?

Chapter 1

Shelley's Heart and Pepys's Lobsters

Biographies are full of verifiable facts, but they are also full of things that aren't there: absences, gaps, missing evidence, knowledge or information that has been passed from person to person, losing credibility or shifting shape on the way. Biographies, like lives, are made up of contested objects—relics, testimonies, versions, correspondences, the unverifiable. What does biography do with the facts that can't be fixed, the things that go missing, the body parts that have been turned into legends and myths?

A few years ago, a popular biographer who had allowed doubts and gaps into the narrative of a historical subject was criticised for sounding dubious. "For 'I think,' read 'I don't know,'" said one of her critics crossly. But more recently, "biographical uncertainty" has become a respectable topic of discussion.[1] Writers on this subject tend to quote Julian Barnes's *Flaubert's Parrot:*

> You can define a net in one of two ways, depending on your point of view. Normally, you would say that it is a meshed instrument designed to catch fish. But you could, with no great injury to logic, reverse the image and define a net as a jocular lexicographer once did: he called it a collection of holes tied together with string.

You can do the same with a biography. The trawling net fills, then the biographer hauls it in, sorts, throws back, stores, fillets and sells. Yet consider what he doesn't catch: there is always far more of that. The biography stands, fat and worthy-burgherish on the shelf, boastful and sedate: a shilling life will give you all the facts, a ten pound one all the hypotheses as well. But think of everything that got away, that fled with the last deathbed exhalation of the biographer.[2]

We all know stories of what falls through the net of biography. Many of these are bonfire stories. The poet, biographer, and editor Ian Hamilton, who had been severely singed in his attempt to write a biography of J. D. Salinger, enjoyed himself in *Keepers of the Flame* (1992) with stories of widows and executors fighting off predatory biographers, of conflagrations of letters, of evidence being withheld. These stories all read like variants of Henry James's novella *The Aspern Papers* in which the predatory would-be biographer, the "publishing scoundrel," is thwarted in his greedy desire to get hold of the papers of the great American romantic poet Jeffrey Aspern by the two protective, solitary women who have inherited and who guard his legacy. These are stories like Byron's executor, publisher, and friends gathering round the fireplace of John Murray's office in Albemarle Street in 1824 and feeding the pages of Byron's memoir into the flames; or Hardy spending six months of 1919 destroying most of his life's papers while setting up a conspiracy with his second wife that she pretend to author the biography he was actually writing himself; or Cassandra Austen destroying those letters of her sister which may have contained revealing personal material; or Elizabeth Gaskell reading, but feeling unable to use, Charlotte Brontë's passionate love-letters to M. Heger, in a biography which set out to protect her against accusations of impurity; or Ted Hughes destroying Sylvia Plath's last two journals, and then publishing his own edition of the rest.

Many literary biographers are affected by such bonfires. Writing on Willa Cather, I came up against her directive, in her will of 1943, that none of her letters should ever be quoted (with the result that they are paraphrased, usually to her disadvantage), alongside her command that no adaptations or dramatisations should be made of her work "whether by electronic means now in existence or which may hereafter be discovered."[3] One of the significant gaps in the Woolf archive is the apparent lack of any correspondence between her and her brother Adrian, so that this relationship has never come into focus. The friendship between Edith Wharton and Henry James is a challenge to her biographers, because James made a bonfire of nearly all the letters he had from her, which as a result have to be decoded from *his* letters to *her*.

James's destruction of Wharton's letters about her private life, or Elizabeth Gaskell's censoring of Charlotte's love letters, are acts of protection, and are often talked about as illustrations—as in *The Aspern Papers*—of the battle for possession that is always fought over a famous literary life. But such disappearances also raise the question of what biographers do with the things that go missing, or with contested objects. Biographers try to make a coherent narrative out of missing documents as well as

existing ones; a whole figure out of body parts. Some
body parts, literally, get into the telling of the stories, in
the form of legends, rumours, or contested possessions.
Body parts are conducive to myth-making; biographers,
in turn, have to sort out the myths from the facts. There
is a tremendous fascination with the bodily relics of
famous people, and the stories of such relics have their
roots in legends and miracles of saints which are the distant ancestors of biography. But they persist in a secular
age, rather in the way that urban myths do, and are some
of the "things" biographers have to decide how to deal
with. These "body-part" stories play into the subject's
posthumous reputation, sometimes with suspicious appo-
siteness. We might expect Joan of Arc's heart (and, it is
sometimes added, her entrails) to have survived the
flames and to have been thrown into the Seine. It seems
fitting, too, that Sir Thomas More's head, boiled, and im-
paled on a pole over London Bridge, is supposed to have
been secretly taken by night by his daughter Margaret
Roper to Saint Dunstan's Church in Canterbury, which,
after the beatification of More in the nineteenth century,
became a pilgrimage shrine. Charlotte Yonge, in *A Book
of Golden Deeds*, retells—without much conviction—the
old story that, in the boat, "Margaret looked up and said:
'That head has often lain in my lap; I would that it would
now fall into it.' And at that moment it actually fell, and
she received it." It's the kind of story probably best ignored by biographers.[4]

There are stranger stories of the fate of relics.
Napoleon's penis is said to have been chopped off by
the Abbé who administered the last rites, and since then
has been sold, inherited, displayed, and auctioned many

times, last heard of in the possession of an American urologist, but possibly buried all this time in the crypt at the Hôtel des Invalides. Hardy's body was interred in Poets' Corner, but, after an argument between his friends and his family, his heart was buried in the grave of his wife, Emma, at Stinsford Church, near Dorchester, carried in an urn to its resting place with great solemnity by a procession of gentlemen in suits and hats (the church has a photograph of the ceremony). On the tomb, it says: "Here Lies The Heart of Thomas Hardy." Rumour has it that Hardy's housekeeper, after the death and the extraction of the heart, placed it in a biscuit tin on the kitchen table, and that when the undertaker came the next day he found an empty biscuit tin and Hardy's cat, Cobby, looking fat and pleased. The story then divides: in one branch a pig's heart replaces Hardy's in the urn. In the other, Cobby is executed by the undertaker and replaces his master's heart. Either way, this rural myth is probably more useful for a *Life of Cobby* than a *Life of Hardy*.[5]

The story of Einstein's brain is intriguingly grotesque, too. After a pathologist from Kansas, Thomas Harvey, performed Einstein's autopsy in 1955, he made off with the brain, claiming he would investigate and publish his findings on it. He cut the brain into 240 pieces, and, at various times, doled out bits to scientific researchers. In 1978 a reporter tracked down Dr. Harvey in Kansas and was shown the brain, kept in two mason jars in a cardboard box. In *Driving Mr. Albert: A Trip across America with Einstein's Brain*, Michael Paterniti described a journey with Dr. Harvey and his "sacred specimen," in which he meditates on the motives for such "relic freaks."[6]

Uncertainty also surrounds the bones of Yeats. Yeats was buried on 30 January 1939 in an Anglican cemetery in France, at Roquebrune. His wife, George, took out a temporary ten-year lease (she thought) on the grave site. Plans to bring his body home to Sligo in September 1939 were thwarted by world events. In 1947, it was discovered that the concession had run out after five years, not ten, and that Yeats's bones had been removed to the ossuary. Very confused negotiations followed between George, some of Yeats's friends, the municipal and church authorities and the French government. In March 1948 the remains were identified (though leaving some room for uncertainty) and placed in a new coffin; in September 1948 the coffin was taken in state from Roquebrune to Galway. The reinterment ceremony at Drumcliff on 17 September 1948 took place with enormous crowds in attendance, and the poet's verse was, some time later, duly inscribed on the tombstone: "Cast a cold eye, on life, on death; Horseman, pass by!" But rumours persisted that the bones had got mixed up in the ossuary; Louis MacNeice, at the funeral, said they were actually burying "a Frenchman with a club foot." Roy Foster's life of Yeats takes a laconic and brisk line on all this, since in his view posthumous legends about body parts have no meaning for the life. "The legend of a mystery burial, or even an empty coffin," he notes dispassionately, "sustains a kind of mythic life, as with King Arthur, or—more appositely—Charles Stewart Parnell." What interests Foster about Yeats's death is that, in the last days, he showed no interest at all in the systems of occultism and supernaturalism that had so preoccupied him, he made no mention of the afterlife, but concentrated exclusively on finishing his last poems. His last conscious act was to "revise a contents list for an imagined last volume of poems."[7]

So, what, if anything, are biographers supposed to do with such mythical body-part stories? They can easily be set aside and ignored. But these compelling relics fit with our deep fascination with deathbed scenes and last words—which I'll come back to in the last essay in this book. We are all fascinated by the manner of the subject's death. And if there are legends about the last moments of the subject, or stories about what happened to their bodies after death—most of which fall into the category of un- verifiable things or contested objects—it is a rare biogra- pher who risks taking no notice of such stories. They play a part in the meaning of the life. How such matters should be dealt with in the biographical narrative involves tricky questions of tone and judgment, often involving a stand- off between scepticism and superstition, rationalism and sentimentalism. But most biographies concern themselves with afterlives as well as with lives.

One of the most complicated and emotionally charged examples in British biography of the contested use of sources, of rival versions and myth-making, in which a body part comes to symbolise the subject's afterlife, is the story of the death of Shelley. Shelley's great biographer Richard Holmes has written several times about this, once in his biography of 1974, once in the chapter called "Exiles," in *Footsteps* (1985), which movingly retraced his own steps as Shelley's biographer, and once in a more re- cent essay on the legends about Shelley that followed his death, in which he notes that "many lives change their

shape as we look back on them."[8] In *Footsteps*, he began
that process of "looking back" on the writing of Shelley's
life by remembering what he had wanted to do as Shelley's
biographer in the 1970s. When he started work, he said,
he was faced with a "received biographical image of Shelley's adult character." This "received image" had "three
powerful components," he added, all of which he wanted
to "explode." One was "the 'angelic' personality of popular myth, the 'Ariel' syndrome, with its strong implication
that Shelley was insubstantial, ineffectual, physically in-
competent." The second "concerned his radical politics,"
which had always been treated "as essentially juvenile, and
incompatible with his mature lyric gift as a writer."
Holmes wanted "to show that Shelley's poetic and political inspirations were closely identified." The third was the
"prevailing attitude" to "Shelley's emotional and sexual
make-up." Holmes cited Matthew Arnold reviewing
Edward Dowden's biography of Shelley in 1886, with horror at what it revealed of the poet's "irregular relations."
Holmes, who described his own experiences and friend-
ships in the 1960s as being rather like those of the Shelley
circle, was not shocked or horrified, and wanted to understand how Shelley's principles of free love and equal part-
nerships could have led to such chaos and suffering.

Matthew Arnold's distaste at Shelley's morals formed
part of a nineteenth- and early twentieth-century story
of posthumous protection and accusation which Holmes
outlined at the start and the end of his Shelley biography. This is how he tells it:

> Shelley's exile, his defection from his class and the disrep-
> utability of his beliefs and behaviour, had a tremendous

effect on the carefully partisan handling of his biography by the survivors of his own circle and generation, and even more so by that of his son's. In the first, the generation of his family and friends, fear of the moral and social stigma attached to many incidents in Shelley's career prevented the publication or even the writing of biographical material until those who were in possession of it, like Hogg, Peacock and Trelawny, were respectable Victorians in their sixties, who were fully prepared to forget, to smudge and to conceal. . . . Mary Shelley was actually prevented from writing anything fuller than [a] brief introduction . . . [and] editorial "Notes" . . . partly by the same considerations of propriety as Shelley's friends, but even more by the fact that Shelley's father, Sir Timothy Shelley of Field Place, specifically forbade any such publications until after his own death . . . and made the ban singularly effective by outliving his detested son by twenty-two years. . . . In the second generation, control of the Shelley papers passed to Boscombe Manor and Sir Percy Florence's wife, Lady Jane Shelley, who made it her life work to establish an unimpeachable feminine and Victorian idealization of the poet. . . . The vetting and control which Lady Jane exercised over the chosen scholars who were allowed into the sanctuary, notably Richard Garnett and Edward Dowden, was strict. . . . This crucial period of Shelley studies was crowned by Edward Dowden's two-volume standard *Life* (1886), whose damaging influence is still powerfully at work in popular estimates of Shelley's writing and character.[9]

Towards the end of the biography, Lady Shelley's shrine at Boscombe Manor is described in more detail as "complete with life-size monument of the poet, lockets of fading hair, glass cases of letters and blue opaque pots containing fragments of bone." Ian Hamilton, in *Keepers of the Flame*, adds Shelley's baby-rattle to the list of sacred items and blames the women for the sanctification of Shelley: Mary was "a pious keeper of her husband's flame." The Shelley scholar Timothy Webb, describing in 1977 the posthumous forces "which operated to thin the poet's blood and to idealise his memory," said that Lady Shelley "kept the poet's hair, his manuscripts (limited access for true believers only), his books and his heart (or was it liver?) which had been rescued from the flames at Viareggio. Before you could enter the shrine you had to remove your hat."[10]

All three of these writers attributed the romanticising of Shelley to Mary Shelley's remorseful, grieving idealisation of her husband, and to the testimonies of Shelley's friends: the egotistical Thomas Jefferson Hogg, the adventurous, self-invented Edward Trelawny, who dined out for years on his Shelley and Byron stories, and the unreliable Leigh Hunt. All of them had their own versions to tell of the end of Shelley's life.

The Shelley story evolved through tremendous battles over materials and versions. Friends and family did battle over "their" accounts of Shelley, censoring each other (Lady Shelley putting a stop to Hogg's biography after two volumes, Trelawny taking issue with Mary's editing of Shelley's work), and changing their own stories. For over a hundred years, accusations and counteraccusations flew of lies, censorship, and even forgery. A splendidly obstreperous book of 1945 by Roger Smith and others, *The Shelley Legend*, much disliked by the Shelley scholars of the time, puts Lady Shelley at the centre of the battle for custody: "Lady Shelley, terrified lest the facts of Shelley's sex-life should become public, made herself the centre of a conspiracy to keep these facts hidden."[11] As Richard Holmes says in his biography, at every point of conflict over the Shelley sources, "where events reveal Shelley in an unpleasant light" (as with his abandonment of Harriet, his first wife, and her subsequent suicide when heavily pregnant) "the original texts and commentaries have attracted suppressions, distortions, and questions of doubtful authenticity, originating from Victorian apologists." William St Clair sums up the matter in his essay of 2002, "The Biographer as Archaeologist": "The general intention of the family was to enhance the reputation of Shelley and of Mary Shelley, and to suppress knowledge of matters which contradicted the image, or rather the myth, which they wanted to see projected . . . for example by removing evidence of irreligion, and slurring . . . the reputation of Shelley's first wife, Harriet." Long after these attempts at censorship, and now that all the facts of Shelley's life have been scrupulously explored, there are still competing versions of the life-story; blame and accusation are still in play.[12]

In a case like Shelley's, the posthumous life of the subject has as much to do with the writing of biography as the life itself. An interesting essay by the critic Andrew Bennett, called "Shelley's Ghosts," touches on this. Bennett argues that Shelley had an acute and intense relation to the idea of posterity, and presents himself in his own work as "a ghostly spirit set to haunt or inhabit the minds of readers." Bennett begins his piece on Shelley as the ghostwriter of his own life by talking about how we treat the dead: "What we do with dead bodies is different

from what we do with live ones."[13] This is particularly
apt for Shelley, since one of the most important ingredients in the making of the Shelley legend was the story of
what happened to Shelley's dead body.

The famous, tragic story, once more. In April 1822, the
Shelleys and their friends moved after a winter in Pisa to
the Casa Magni, at Lerici on the Gulf of Spezia. The
household consisted of Percy and Mary Shelley and little
Percy, Claire Clairmont, and Jane and Edward Williams.
Claire's daughter by Byron, Allegra, died in April. Mary,
two of whose children had died, had a miscarriage in
July; both women were ill and distressed. Byron and his
flamboyant entourage were at the Palazzo Lanfranchi in
Pisa. Leigh Hunt and his family were arriving in July;
there was a plan that Hunt, Byron, and Shelley should
start a magazine. Shelley was writing *The Triumph of Life*,
Byron was writing *Don Juan*. Byron and Shelley, with the
advice and help of their new friend, the swashbuckling,
self-invented Edward Trelawny, and a Captain Roberts,
had become addicted to sailing. Byron was having a large
schooner built, the *Bolivar*; Shelley's smaller boat was
called the *Don Juan*, though he had wanted to call it
Ariel. In June, it was refurbished, by some accounts un-
wisely, with new topmast rigging.

Shelley and Edward Williams and Captain Roberts
sailed on the *Don Juan* down the coast to meet Leigh
Hunt, newly arrived at Leghorn (Livorno), on 1 July
1822, to help them get settled in Pisa. On 8 July, Shelley,
Williams, and the ship-boy, Charles Vivian, set sail from
Livorno to return to Lerici, on a stormy day. A squall
broke out in the Gulf of Spezia, the *Don Juan* went down

under full sail, and they were all drowned. The women were waiting for them at the Casa Magni. It took another ten days of agonised and confused waiting and searching, in which Trelawny played a leading part, before the bodies were washed up and the news of the deaths was confirmed. The bodies were buried in quicklime on the shore to avoid infection. On 13 August, after getting permission from the authorities, Trelawny, Byron, and Hunt, with soldiers, attendants, and onlookers, dug up Williams's body and burnt it on a pyre; on 14 August they repeated the ceremony for Shelley, on the beach at Viareggio.

The telling of this story formed a central part in the making of the Shelley legend, and it was seized upon with gusto by the main players. Here is part of Trelawny's 1858 version, written thirty-six years after the event. It has been variously described as "a semi-fictionalized account," "one of the great purple passages of romantic literature, and deservedly so," and "a scene which in all its gruesome detail has etched itself onto the Romantic imagination":[14]

> The first indication of their having found the body, was the appearance of the end of a black silk handkerchief . . . then some shreds of linen were met with, and a boot with the bone of the leg and the foot in it. On the removal of a layer of brushwood all that now remained of my lost friend was exposed—a shapeless mass of bones and flesh. The limbs separated from the trunk on being touched.
>
> "Is that a human body?" exclaimed Byron; "why it's more like the carcase of a sheep, or any other animal, than a man: this is a satire on our pride and folly."

I pointed to the letters E.E.W. on the black silk handkerchief.

Byron, looking on, muttered: "The entrails of a worm hold together longer than the potter's clay, of which man is made. Hold! Let me see the jaw," he added, as they were removing the skull, "I can recognize anyone by the teeth, with whom I have talked. I always watch the lips and mouth: they tell what the tongue and eye try to conceal."

. . . [Williams's] remains were removed piecemeal into the furnace.

"Don't repeat this with me," said Byron, "let my carcase rot where it falls."

The funereal pyre was now ready; I applied the fire, and the materials being dry and resinous the pine-wood burnt furiously, and drove us back. . . . As soon as the flames became clear, and allowed us to approach, we threw frankincense and salt into the furnace, and poured a flask of wine and oil over the body. The Greek oration was omitted, for we had lost our Hellenic bard. It was now so insufferably hot that the officers and soldiers were all seeking shade.

"Let us try the strength of these waters that drowned our friends," said Byron, with his usual audacity. "How far out do you think they were when their boat sank?"

"If you don't wish to be put into the furnace, you had better not try; you are not in condition."

He stripped, and went into the water, and so did I and my companion. Before we got a mile out Byron was sick, and persuaded to return to the shore.

The lonely and grand scenery that surrounded us so exactly harmonized with Shelley's genius, that I could imagine his spirit soaring over us. . . . As I thought of the delight Shelley felt in such scenes of loneliness and grandeur whilst living, I felt we were no better than a herd of wolves or a pack of wild dogs, in tearing out his battered and naked body from the pure yellow sand that lay so lightly over it, to drag him back to the light of day. . . . Even Byron was silent and thoughtful. We were startled and drawn together by a dull hollow sound that followed the blow of a mattock; the iron had struck a skull, and the body was soon removed. Lime had been strewn on it; this, or decomposition, had the effect of staining it of a dark and ghastly indigo colour. Byron asked me to preserve the skull for him; but remembering that he had formerly used one as a drinking-cup, I was determined Shelley's should not be so profaned. The limbs did not separate from the trunk, as in the case of Williams's body, so that the corpse was removed entire into the furnace. . . . More wine was poured over Shelley's dead body than he had consumed during his life. This with the oil and salt made the yellow flames glisten and quiver. . . . The corpse fell open and the heart was laid bare. The frontal bone of the skull, where it had been struck with the mattock, fell off; and, as the back of the head rested on the red-hot bottom bars of the furnace, the brains literally seethed, bubbled, and boiled as in a cauldron, for a very long time.

Byron could not face this scene, he withdrew to the beach and swam off to the *Bolivar*. Leigh Hunt remained in the carriage. . . . The only portions that were not consumed were some fragments of bones, the jaw, and the

skull, but what surprised us all, was that the heart remained entire. In snatching this relic from the fiery furnace my hand was severely burnt; and had any one seen
me do the act I should have been put into quarantine.

After cooling the iron machine in the sea, I collected
the human ashes and placed them in a box, which I took
on board the *Bolivar.* Byron and Hunt retraced their steps
to their home, and the officers and soldiers returned to
their quarters.[15]

No reader can fail to be struck by Trelawny's highly
coloured Hamlet-ising of Byron; the deliberate contrast
between Byron's worldliness, appetites, and cynicism, and
Shelley's ethereality (which goes all through Trelawny's
memoir); the pathetic fallacy which invests the scenery
with the spirit of Shelley's genius; the pagan quality of the
event (no prayers, Greek libations), and—not least—the
emphasis on Trelawny as the main, heroic protagonist
and the only true witness (the others either wandering off
or averting their faces). It comes as no surprise to hear
that Trelawny was given to showing off the scars he got
from plunging his hand and arm into the fire.

This was not Trelawny's first, or his last, version of
the scene. His latest biographer, David Crane, notes: "In
account after account over the next sixty years he would
return to this summer of 1822 with ever new details, ped-
dling scraps of history or bones with equal relish."[16]
Holmes says that he "obsessively re-wrote his account
nearly a dozen times over the next fifty years, accumulat-
ing more and more baroque details, like some sinister biographical coral-reef." Each version became less realistic
than its predecessor. As the retellings developed, "the

physical details became gradually less gruesome . . . and . . . the romantic setting which had originally been the back-drop to the cremation of Williams, was later transferred to the cremation of the Poet."[17] In versions written in 1822, he tells us that Williams's body had "the eyes out" and was "fish-eaten," and that Shelley's body "was in a stage of putridity and very offensive. Both the legs were separated at the knee-joint . . . the hands were off and the arm bones protruding—the skull black and no flesh or features of the face remaining. . . . The flesh was of a dingy blue." The later version that I've quoted, the one published in 1858, altered and prettified the story for "his more squeamish Victorian contemporaries." When Trelawny returned to the story yet again in 1878, he em-bellished further, with details such as these: "Shelley . . . had a black single-breasted jacket on, with an outside pocket as usual on each side of his jacket. When his body was washed on shore, Aeschylus was in his left pocket, and Keats's last poems was in his right, doubled back, as thrust away in the exigency of the moment."[18]

Confusion developed over whether he had seen the bodies when they were first washed up; over what hap-pened to the body of Charles Vivian; over whether Byron actually witnessed the burning of Shelley's body or not; over whether it was a volume of Aeschylus or Sophocles in the left pocket; over which page of Keats's last poems the book was doubled back at—was it "Lamia," or "Isabella," or "The Eve of St Agnes?"—or whether anything survived of the volume except its cov-ers; and, of course, over the size of Shelley's heart.

But, notoriously unreliable though they were, such firsthand versions made their way irresistibly into the biographies of Shelley. Trelawny's witness was compounded by that of Leigh Hunt, an even more emotional narrative, with a convincingly ironic coda:

> The ceremony of the burning was alike beautiful and distressing. Trelawny . . . [took] the most active part on this last mournful occasion. He and his friend Captain Shenley were first upon the ground, attended by proper assistants. Lord Byron and myself arrived shortly afterwards. His lordship got out of his carriage, but wandered away from the spectacle, and did not see it. I remained inside the carriage, now looking on, now drawing back with feelings that were not to be witnessed.

> None of the mourners, however, refused themselves the little comfort of supposing, that lovers of books and antiquity, like Shelley and his companion, Shelley in particular with his Greek enthusiasm, would not have been sorry to foresee this part of their fate. The mortal part of him, too, was saved from corruption; not the least extraordinary part of his history. Among the materials for burning, as many of the gracefuller and more classical articles as could be procured—frankincense, wine, etc—were not forgotten; and to these Keats's volume was added. The beauty of the flame arising from the funeral pile was extraordinary. The weather was beautifully fine. The Mediterranean, now soft and lucid, kissed the shore as if to make peace with it . . . the flame of the fire bore away towards heaven in vigorous amplitude, waving and quivering with a brightness of inconceivable beauty. It seemed as though it contained the glassy essence of vitality. You might have expected a seraphic countenance to look out of it, turning once more before it departed, to thank the friends that had done their duty.

Yet, see how extremes can appear to meet even on occasions the most overwhelming. . . . On returning from one of our visits to the seashore, we dined and drank; I mean, Lord Byron and myself; dined little, and drank too much. . . . I had bordered upon emotions which I have never suffered myself to indulge. . . . The barouche drove rapidly through the forest of Pisa. We sang, we laughed, we shouted. I even felt a gaiety the more shocking, because it was real and a relief.[19]

Such "eyewitness" accounts, along with other testimonies from Thomas Love Peacock (written forty years after the event), Byron, and Hogg, powerfully influenced the earliest full biography (written under the sanitising control of Lady Shelley). Edward Dowden, for his part, relied heavily on Trelawny and Hunt, though he censors the inappropriate scene of Hunt and Byron returning to Pisa roaring drunk. He takes from Trelawny's later version the added detail that Shelley's heart was "unusually large," and a conveniently symbolic sea-bird, which in some versions was a curlew, in others a seagull, with (as one of Trelawny's editors put it) "a ghastly unappeased appetite for roast poet."[20]

The furnace being placed and surrounded by wood, the remains were removed from their shallow resting-place. It was Byron's wish that the skull, which was of unusual beauty, should be preserved; but it almost instantly fell to pieces. Of the volume of Keats's poems which had been buried with Shelley's body, only the binding remained, and this was cast upon the pyre. . . . Three hours elapsed before [the body] separated; it then fell open across the breast; the heart, which was unusually large, seemed

impregnable to the fire. Trelawny plunged his hand into
the flames and snatched this relic from the burning. The
day was one of wide autumnal calm and beauty. . . . During the whole funeral ceremony a solitary sea-bird crossing and recrossing the pile was the only intruder that baf-
fled the vigilance of the guard.

Byron, who could not face the scene, had swum off to
his yacht. Leigh Hunt looked on from the carriage. Having cooled the furnace in the sea, Trelawny collected the
fragments of bones and the ashes, and deposited them in
the oaken box. All was over. Byron and Hunt returned to
Pisa in their carriage. Shenley and Trelawny, bearing the
oaken coffer, went on board the *Bolivar*. The relics of
Shelley's heart, given soon after by Trelawny to Hunt,
were, at Mary Shelley's urgent request, supported by the
entreaty of Mrs Williams, confided to Mary's hands. After
her death, in a copy of the Pisa edition of "Adonais," at
the page which tells how death is swallowed up by immortality, was found under a silken covering the embrowned
ashes, now shrunk and withered, which she had secretly
treasured.[21]

Dowden takes us on to the next stage of the narrative,
the quarrel over the possession of Shelley's heart. And
what happened to Shelley's heart became, like everything
else to do with his death, a source of controversy. There
appears to have been an unseemly and passionate tussle
over the heart between Trelawny, Hunt, and Mary
Shelley. John Gisborne, Maria Gisborne's husband, gave
one version of the quarrel in one of the hundreds of documents which form the huge compilation of Shelley
materials made by Lady Shelley.

After the funeral rites of Shelley had been performed . . . Trelawny gave the heart, which had remained unconsumed, to Hunt. Mary wrote to Hunt requesting that it might be sent to her. Hunt refused to part with it. . . . Mary was in despair. At length the amiable Mrs Williams . . . wrote to Hunt, and represented to him how grievous and melancholy it was that Shelley's remains should become a source of dissension between his dearest friends.[22]

Articles were written with titles like "The Real Truth about Shelley's Heart." Frederick Jones, the first editor of Mary Shelley's letters and journals, summed up the controversy in his edition of the letters in the 1930s:

Much controversy has raged about Shelley's heart. . . . That Trelawny did remove the heart and that it was kept by Mary, there can be no doubt . . . Mary's, Hunt's, and Byron's letters, and other evidence are quite conclusive. After Mary's death Sir Percy and Lady Shelley kept it, and at the death of Sir Percy in 1890 it was placed in his coffin and buried with him in St Peter's Churchyard at Bournemouth.[23]

The battle over the possession of Shelley's heart seems to embody the contest over who should "own" Shelley's story. That it was given reluctantly into Mary Shelley's hands by Shelley's male friends points to Mary's position in the posthumous life of her husband. Mary's biographer Miranda Seymour, who set out to defend Mary against what she saw as a concerted effort to sideline and denigrate her by Shelley's friends and biographers (including Holmes, whose picture of Mary Shelley, according to Seymour, is of a "sulky, nagging wife"), gives a partisan account of Mary's role in the events:

> As his bones shrivelled to ashes on the shore, Mary's relationship with Shelley was already being judged. No precious relic was brought back for her from the funeral pyre. This was the age in which, without photographs . . . fragments of the dead were invested with the value of talismans. Byron's choice, the skull, fell to pieces in the flames. Trelawny burned his hands in seizing a fragment of jawbone; Hunt took another. The heart, or the part of the remains which seemed most like a heart, had failed to burn, while exuding a viscous liquid. [Seymour's footnote to this sentence reads: *The heart's survival in intense heat is hard to explain, even if it had been in an advanced state of calcification. It is possible that the object snatched from the flame was the poet's liver.*] Trelawny snatched it out; Hunt requested and received [it]. When Mary asked if she might have the heart herself, Hunt refused to surrender it. . . . It took a reproachful letter from Jane Williams to Hunt to compel a surrender. The heart was rediscovered after Mary Shelley's death. Wrapped in silk between the pages of *Adonais*, it had lain inside her travelling-desk for almost thirty years.
>
> . . . The task of defending and enhancing her husband's reputation would be her great work for the future, her consolation for the remorse she now felt.[24]

Clearly, the battle for possession over Shelley's heart—if it was his heart—has not come to an end.

Mary Shelley's letters at the time of Shelley's death to their mutual friend Maria Gisborne immediately began the process of Shelley's idealisation, on which Holmes has commented: "The legend of his death transformed his life almost beyond recovery."[25] In this process, Shelley's elegy for Keats came to be read as his own elegy, and his soul was felt to have an ethereal life beyond his death. For Mary, Shelley's heart at once took on the mythical resonance it has continued to have since then, as the "unconsumable" immortal part of the poet.

> Today—this day—the sun shining in the sky—they are gone to the desolate sea coast to perform the last offices to their earthly remains. Hunt, L[ord] B[yron] & Trelawny. The quarantine laws would not permit us to remove them sooner—& now only on condition that we burn them to ashes. . . . Adonais is not Keats's it is his own elegy. . . . I have seen the spot where he now lies—the sticks that mark the spot where the sands cover him . . .—They are now about this fearful office—& I live!
>
> I will say nothing of the ceremony since Trelawny has written an account of it. . . . I will only say that all except his heart (which was unconsumable) was burnt, and that two days ago I went to Leghorn and beheld the small box that contained his earthly dross—that form, those smiles—Great God! No he is not there—he is with me, about me—life of my life & soul of my soul—if his divine spirit did not penetrate mine I could not survive to weep thus.[26]

That spiritualised Shelley would inspire such romantic versions as André Maurois's *Ariel: A Shelley Romance*, of 1924, translated by Ella d'Arcy, and highly popular in its time, where Shelley's soul is "clipt in a net woven of dew-dreams," his blood is always freezing and his heart is forever standing still or pounding in his breast. And the sacred heart of Mary's, kept in the pages of *Adonais*, is a perfect example of a contested body part whose possession and appropriation can stand in for the whole biographical history of the subject. Writing desolately in her journal for 11 November 1822, after she has been accused (by Leigh Hunt) of coldheartedness, Mary cries out:

> A cold heart! have I [a] cold heart? . . . Yes! it would be cold enough if all were as I wished it—cold, or burning in that flame for whose sake I forgive this, and would forgive every other imputation—that flame in which your heart, Beloved one, lay unconsumed! Where are you, Shelley? . . . My heart is very full tonight. . . . I shall write his life.[27]

That heartfelt quotation seems uncannily to sum up the biographer's question. *"Where are you, Shelley?"* Who do you belong to? Who "owns" your "unconsumed" heart? Mary's possessive lament can be set against another act of posthumous appropriation, carried out by Trelawny in the Protestant Cemetery at Rome. Trelawny's "management" of Shelley's tomb is another gripping story in itself. Joseph Severn, sadly taking care of the plans for his own friend Keats's tombstone, was suddenly confronted with the extraordinary figure of Trelawny, whom he described in a fine letter of April 1823 as this "cockney-corsair," this "pair of Mustachios," "this Lord Byron's Jackal."[28] Trelawny completely took over, insisted on moving Shelley's ashes to a site nearer to Keats's grave, with a space for Trelawny right next to Shelley, and chose the wording for the tombstone. At the top, he had the words "Cor Cordium" engraved. (Frederick Jones, Mary Shelley's editor, visiting the grave in the 1930s, noted that "Roman tourist guides, pointing to 'Cor Cordium' on the tombstone, tell travellers that the heart lies under the stone.") Beneath them were the lines from *The Tempest*:

> Nothing of him that doth fade
> But doth suffer a sea change
> Into something rich and strange.

"Rich and strange" indeed is the posthumous life of Shelley. But Richard Holmes, in his biography, would have none of all this. He calls Mary's identification of "Adonais" with Shelley, rather than with Keats, a "sentimental half-truth" and he will have no truck with any of the versions of Shelley's death I have been describing. This is how he tells the story:

> The bodies of Shelley, Edward Williams, and Charles Vivian were eventually washed up along the beach between Massa and Viareggio ten days after the storm. The exposed flesh of Shelley's arms and face had been entirely eaten away, but he was identifiable by the nankeen trousers, the white silk socks beneath the boots and Hunt's copy of Keats's poems doubled back in the jacket pocket. To comply with the complicated quarantine laws, Trelawny had the body temporarily buried in the sand with quick lime, and dug up again on 15 August to be placed in a portable iron furnace that had been constructed to his specification at Livorno, and burnt on the beach in the presence of Leigh Hunt, Lord Byron, some Tuscan militia and a few local fishermen. Much later Shelley's ashes were buried in a tomb, also designed by Trelawny, in the Protestant Cemetery at Rome, after

having remained for several months in a mahogany chest in the British Consul's wine-cellar.

In England, the news of Shelley's death was first published by the *Examiner* on 4 August, and on the following evening by the *Courier* whose article began: "Shelley, the writer of some infidel poetry has been drowned; *now* he knows whether there is a God or no."[29]

Shelley's heart is a deliberate gap here, a body part that goes missing in the interests of dealing with a particular problem in literary biography, and as a way of getting out of a biographical trap, in which, as Holmes put it many years later, "biography is caught and frozen, so to speak, in the glamorous headlights of Shelley's death."[30]

To turn from the story of Shelley to the story of Pepys is to make a grotesquely violent jump from tragedy to comedy, from the ethereal to the robust, and from posthumous myth-making to material realities. Pepys's story is simply steaming with body parts and objects of consumption, from the bosoms and bottoms he so loved to fondle, to the Parmesan cheese he made sure to bury in his garden during the Great Fire of London. Pepys's most dramatic "body-part" story is not one of a heart magically unconsumed by the flames, but of a gall stone painfully extracted without anaesthetic. The life of Pepys would seem to raise none of the problems of missing parts and contested legends raised by the death of Shelley. Instead, it provokes a feeling we may have about life-writing which was most brilliantly articulated by the fin-de-siècle French man of letters, Marcel Schwob. In his

Vies Imaginaires of 1896 (well ahead of Lytton Strachey) he argued that short lives (preferably of obscure characters) are more revealing than long lives of great men, and that what is most revealing are the quirks, the eccentricities, and the body parts. History books only ever deal with such body parts if they are thought to have had a determining effect on "general events":

> [History tells us] that Napoleon was in pain on the day of Waterloo . . . that Alexander was drunk when he killed Klitos, and that certain of Louis XIV's shifts of policy may have been caused by his fistula. Pascal speculates about how things might have turned out had Cleopatra's nose been shorter, and about the grain of sand in Cromwell's urethra. All these individual facts are important only because they have influenced events.

But biographies can do more, Schwob argues, with oddities and idiosyncrasies, than "historical science" can:

> That such-a-one had a crooked nose, that he had one eye higher than the other, that he had rheumatic nodules in the joints of his arm, that at such-an-hour he customarily ate a *blanc-de-poulet*, that he preferred Malvoisie to Château Margaux—there is something unparalleled in all the world. Thales might just as well have said [Know thyself] as Socrates; but he would not have rubbed his leg in the same way, in prison, before drinking the hemlock.[31]

Claire Tomalin, Pepys's most recent and most praised biographer, rather than trying to deal with unverifiable legends, has the pleasure of plunging into all those kinds of oddities and idiosyncrasies, in a life full to the brim with authentic, factual, bodily, everyday materials. She makes the most of the body parts: the most brilliant, and appalling, set piece in her book is the detailed account of the excruciating operation for the removal of that bladder-stone. Pepys kept his stone, had a special case made for it, and showed it to his friends. (Perhaps it survived him, like Napoleon's penis.) His mother, who had the same condition and "voided" her stone, threw hers on the fire. Tomalin points to this as the crucial difference between the "classifying" and "purposeful" son and his "sluttish," "tough" old mother. She enjoys Pepys's ambition and orderliness, his endless enthusiasm for and curiosity about himself, and his pleasure in ordinary human activity, from hearing fine music to eating a good dinner to designing a new bookcase. And she relishes the openness, curiosity, plain-speaking and dramatic immediacy of the Diary: a diary which might be enough to make any biographer feel redundant.[32]

Sex, drink, plague, fire, city life, music, plays, marital conflict, the fall of kings, loyalty and betrayal, ambition, corruption and courage in public life, wars, navies, public executions, incarceration in the Tower: Samuel Pepys's life is full of irresistible material. His famously candid, minute, and inexhaustibly vigorous account of every detail of his daily life filled six leather-bound books written in shorthand. The unpublished nineteenth-century transcription ran to fifty-four volumes; the definitive edition by Robert Latham and William Matthews is in eleven volumes. (The story of the Diary's survival and publication is in itself a remarkable one.) But the Diary, which begins on 1 January 1660 and ends (because of Pepys's eye problems) on 31 May 1669, covers only nine years out of a seventy-year life. The twenty-seven-year story that precedes it—of Pepys's family, childhood, education, professional advancement, and marriage, in the context of the Civil War—and the thirty-four years that follow it, when the death of his wife and public disgrace were followed by rehabilitation, distinguished years of naval administration, an active retirement after 1688, and a second long relationship, all have to be tracked without the Diary. This silence is filled by a vast mass of materials: thousands of letters, Pepys's work-papers and trial documents, naval histories (including Pepys's own), Admiralty papers, contemporary diaries and memoirs, and many histories and biographies. Yet it also involves, as Tomalin puts it, much "obscurity and guesswork."[33]

Claire Tomalin had two challenges to overcome with Pepys. One is that the Diary provides so much material it is sometimes overpowering. The other is that outside the Diary-years, and outside Pepys's own point of view, she has to hypothesise. As in her Lives of Jane Austen and Dickens's mistress Ellen Ternan (*The Invisible Woman*), she often has to proceed by ingenious analogies. Since we don't know how Pepys was brought up, she provides a contemporary manual of manners for children from 1577. Since we don't have first-hand accounts of the sexual activities of young men-about-town in the 1650s, she points us to a book of advice on *The Arts of Wooing and Complementing*, written by Milton's nephew in 1658. In filling the gaps, Tomalin characteristically brings some sympathetic guesswork to the voiceless heroines of Pepys's story—maids, mistresses, patronesses—and especially to his wife, Elizabeth Pepys, the beautiful, penniless, quick-tempered French girl whom Pepys married when she was nearly fifteen. Tomalin makes her the

"muse" of the Diary: Pepys is "inspired" to write it "by
the condition of marriage itself."[34]

But for all his alluring openness and the mass of evidence he provides, Pepys raises some strategic problems
for his biographer. If she paraphrases him, as she must,
what goes missing? A few tiny examples of the transition
from diary to biography show how the source-material
has to be tidied up, little bits of it lopped off here and
there, in order to give the life-story a clear narrative
shape.

Tomalin describes Pepys inviting Elizabeth to join
him on a trip to the residence of his patrons at Hunting-
don on 13 September 1663, "with the gallant words":
"Well, shall you and I never travel together again?" "As
soon as they arrived at Brampton," Tomalin continues,
"he took her to spend the day with Lady Sandwich.
Later they rode into the woods to gather nuts, and he
showed her the river." She calls this an "idyllic . . . afternoon together in the autumn sunshine." In the Diary,
this trip is more of a mess. After his invitation to her,
they don't in fact set out together, but ride out sepa-
rately, as he has to wait for someone else. They meet up
on the way, and Elizabeth is taken ill drinking beer, and
is alarmingly sick. When they arrive at Brampton they
are extremely tired. Pepys visits Lady Sandwich on his
own, not with his wife, and then leaves Elizabeth behind
when he returns to town. It isn't until 19 September, a
week later, that they go riding in Brampton woods, eating nuts in the sunshine, and it's she who shows him
the river "behind my father's house," not the other way
round. Elsewhere in the biography, Tomalin does refer
to Pepys's anxiety at Elizabeth's sickness while riding

to Brampton, but she doesn't link the two occasions
together.[35]

Wanting to show his mixed feelings about death,
Tomalin reports the dream Pepys has after his mother's
death. "He dreamt of her again, coming to him and asking for a pair of gloves, and in the dream 'thinking it to
be a mistake in our thinking her all this while dead.'"
She quotes him again: "This dream troubled me and I
waked." But in the Diary, this is followed by further
nightmares: of seeing his urine turning into a turd, or of
pulling at something, possibly from the end of his penis,
that looked like "snot or slime," and this substance turning into "a gray kind of bird . . . [that] run from me to
the corner of the door." This is horrifying to him. But
Tomalin—though far from squeamish—doesn't quote
this, perhaps because she is more concerned at this point
to draw an analogy between Pepys's dream of his dead
mother and Proust's dream of his dead grandmother.
(Tomalin frequently compares Pepys to Proust, and she
starts her book with Proust's epigram: "Un livre est le
produit d'un autre moi que celui que nous manifestons
dans nos habitudes, dans la société, dans nos vices." But
Pepys's Diary is surely the product of exactly the "moi,"
the self, which *does* manifest itself in its habits, social life,
and vices.)[36]

Here is one last little example of an oddity that has
been tidied up in paraphrase. On 13 June 1666, Pepys
was saying grace at dinner. In the middle, he says, "my
mind fell upon my lobsters," and he jumps up, exclaim-
ing, "Cud Zookes! What is become of my lobsters!" He
had bought two fine ones that day, but had left them in a
hackney coach. Tomalin mentions this twice, once to

show how Pepys likes to repeat his own sayings, once to display his extraordinary energy. On the same day he loses the lobsters, he also attends the funeral of Admiral Myngs, goes to a board meeting in Whitehall, visits the Exchequer and the studio of a painter who is doing a portrait of his father, and goes to his mistress in Deptford where he "did what he would with her." He gets a boat home, drinks a pint of sack, and buys three eels from a fisherman. No wonder he forgot his lobsters! But what Claire Tomalin omits is that he remembers that he forgot them, and bursts out with his exclamation, in the middle of saying grace.[37] (And perhaps that's why he writes it down: he may have been rather ashamed of himself, and wanted to expiate the offence in the Diary.) The story has been slightly flattened, and has lost a little of its idiosyncrasy. But the biographer can't do everything. Biography has to omit and to choose. In the process, some things go missing—in this case, just the whiskers of a pair of crustaceans that fell through the gaps in the net.

....

Chapter 2

Virginia Woolf's Nose

Biography is a process of making up, or making over. The *New Oxford Dictionary of English* (2001) includes in its definitions of "making up": "to compose or constitute a whole (of parts)"; "to put together or prepare something (like mortar) from parts or ingredients"; "to arrange type and illustrations on a page"; and "to concoct or invent a story." "Making over" has two meanings: "to transfer the possession of something to someone," and "to completely transform or remodel something" (such as a person's hairstyle—or nose). Since biographers try to compose a whole out of parts (evidence, testimony, stories, chronologies) and arrange it on the page, since they appropriate their subjects and usually attempt to create a new or special version of them (so that we speak of Edel's James or Ellmann's Joyce), and since they must give a quasi-fictional, storylike shape to their material (or no one will read them), these terms seem to fit. But pulling against "making up" or "making over," both of which imply some forms of alteration or untruth, is the responsibility to likeness and the need for accuracy.

At a conference on biography in London in the 1990s, when various practitioners (myself included) were holding forth on the ambiguities and relativity of biography, the biographer of a philosopher rose to his feet and said: "But there is such a thing as a fact."[1] Once we get to anything less well-attested than a time and a date for tea written in a person's diary, or the outbreak of the First World War, most biographical facts are open to interpretation. But they do exist, and lie around biographers in huge files and boxes, waiting to be turned into story. These facts have owners: they belong to the lives of the biographer's subject and the people whom the subject knew, loved, hated, worked with or brought up, or perhaps met once in the street in passing. All these people will feel a claim over the fact that concerns them. My first experience of being on the receiving end of this was to read, in a biography of my friend the novelist Brian Moore, that I and my husband got lost on our way to visit Brian and Jean Moore at their remote house in Nova Scotia in the mid-1990s, and had to spend the night in a hotel. No such thing happened, and—although this "fact" didn't have the slightest bearing on Brian Moore's story, except as a useful way of describing how out-of-the-way his house was—I felt a twinge of outrage and bafflement on reading it, as though a tiny part of my life had been forever traduced. I imagined, then, what it might be like (as for Ted Hughes, for instance) to feel that one's whole life had been falsely "made over" by biographers: hence his despairing, angry, and futile cry: "I hope each one of us owns the facts of his or her own life."[2] No: for the biographised and for their friends and family, there is a fight from the death over facts, between the participants in a life and the writers of it.[3] And even if, unusually, no such tug-of-war takes place, the biographer still has to have the internal tussle between "making up" and "fact," or "making over" and "likeness."

No wonder that such strong emotions of blame and anger can circulate around biography, or that it is likely to be seen, in the worst cases, as a form of betrayal. For those with an investment in a life-story (whether as relatives, descendants, friends, lovers, colleagues, admirers, scholars, or devoted readers) a kind of despair can be felt if what's judged to be an inauthentic version of the life gains currency and prevails. Virginia Woolf provides a particularly interesting example here, because—like Sylvia Plath, or Shelley, or Jane Austen—her life and work have been, since her death, variously and passionately idealised, vilified, fictionalised, and mythologised. (An eventful life is not a prerequisite for such passionate make-overs.) Now that this much contested literary life-story has been turned into novel and film, a powerful popularised version of her, for the time being, prevails. In this version, biography and fiction have become blurred together to produce an image of Virginia Woolf which has aroused some anger in those who feel she has been thereby betrayed. I want to look in some detail at this recent making up, or making over, of Woolf, and to ask what these reinterpretations (the technical term is "versionings") suggest to us about her influence and her afterlife, and about the processes of telling a life-story.

At the beginning of the film *The Hours* (2003; written by David Hare, directed by Stephen Daldry, and based on the novel by Michael Cunningham), we hear in voice-over the words of Virginia Woolf's suicide note to her husband, Leonard, and we see Nicole Kidman as Woolf, looking young and fierce, writing the note, leaving her country house (on a beautiful summer day), walking determinedly, in a tweed coat, down the garden path and towards the river-bank, and slowly entering, until she is fully immersed, the green, sun-and-shade-dappled waters of a gently flowing river, to the accompaniment of birds calling and a pulsating, emotional score by Philip Glass. Since the film begins with this romanticised version of the suicide of Virginia Woolf, it sets up a life-story which is moving inexorably towards that death. In the next moment that we see her, she is starting to write *Mrs Dalloway*, so that to a casual audience the two things—her writing of the novel and her suicide—might seem to be going on at the same time. As the story of *Mrs Dalloway* unfolds in her mind, it is entirely about the choice between life and death. The other two narratives in the film, which has three intercut story-lines, are also concerned with that choice.

I noticed a tiny pause in the voice-over at the start of *The Hours*, which took me back to the work I did on my biography of Woolf, one of the sources used by Cunningham and, later, by the filmmakers. When I read the manuscript of her suicide notes to Leonard (she wrote two versions for him, and one for her sister Vanessa, unable to stop revising her work until the very end), with those heartbreaking phrases ("I feel certain that I am going mad again: I feel we can't go through another of those terrible times. . . . You have given me the greatest possible happiness . . ."),[4] I was struck by the organisation of the words on the page. Woolf had written them in short, jagged half-lines, as if she could hardly get to the end of the sentences. I reproduced the letter in my book as it looked on her page, almost like a poem.

Michael Cunningham reprinted it in the same way in his novel. As we hear Kidman speaking the words at the start of the film, and see her writing them, she hesitates, almost imperceptibly, on one of those line-breaks, as if she can't quite go on.

The process of creative translation that stretches from Virginia Woolf writing that letter over sixty years ago to Nicole Kidman playing her character with award-winning, long-nosed intensity is a long and complex one. It layers Woolf's 1925 novel *Mrs Dalloway* with Cunningham's novel (the surprise American literary hit and Pulitzer Prize–winner of 1999), with David Hare's screenplay for and Stephen Daldry's direction of the film of *The Hours*. I think Woolf would have been intrigued by this process. *Mrs Dalloway* (as Elaine Showalter has noted)[5] is an extremely cinematic novel. Woolf was showing an interest at this time in the cinema as a new medium which could express emotions—like fear—without words. She wrote an essay on this in 1926, after going to see *The Cabinet of Dr. Caligari*: "It seems plain that the cinema has within its grasp innumerable symbols for emotions that have so far failed to find expression. . . . The most fantastic contrasts could be flashed before us with a speed which the writer can only toil after in vain." However, in her enthusiasm for the new form, she notes that the results of adapting famous novels for the screen are "disastrous to both." Take *Anna Karenina* (of which she must have seen a 1920s, pre-Garbo film version). In the film, we just see her "teeth, her pearls, and her velvet," and scenes of her kissing Vronsky "with enormous succulence, great deliberation, and infinite gesticulation on a sofa in an extremely well-appointed library, while a gardener incidentally mows the lawn." In the book, "we know Anna almost entirely by the inside of her mind." "So we lurch and lumber through one of the most famous novels of the world."[6] A salutary warning, you might think, for the adapters of a novel that itself "adapted" and "rewrote" *Mrs Dalloway*.

Mrs Dalloway was the ideal novel through which to fictionalise the life of Virginia Woolf, because it is itself so much about life-writing. Early on in the novel, the aeroplane above the Mall, which the citizens of postwar, peacetime London gaze up at wonderingly and happily, loops its advertisement in the sky, writing a different message for each of them ("But what letters? A C was it? an E, then an L? Only for a moment did they lie still. . . . 'Glaxo . . .' 'Kreemo . . .' . . . 'It's toffee,' murmured Mr. Bowley"). To the hallucinating shell-shock victim Septimus Smith, the words in the sky seem to be a signal directed at him, though "he could not read the language yet."[7] Everyone in the novel has an unreadable life secreted inside, in layer upon layer of memory, emotion, habit, thought, and response, which the language of the novel burrows down into and excavates, but which can only be glimpsed on the surface in the simplified single letters by which we recognise each other externally. Mrs. Dalloway's maxim is that "she would not say of any one in the world now that they were this or were that." The novel describes people living extremely complex and volatile interior lives, and breaking through to occasional moments of recognition, of which the most intimate, and unlikely, is the society lady and Tory MP's wife Clarissa Dalloway's understanding of Septimus

Smith's life and death (though he knows nothing at all
about hers).

Woolf's working title for the novel was "The Hours"
(which Cunningham takes as his title), and her notes to
herself about the writing of "The Hours" include this
passage (which Cunningham uses as his epigraph):

> I should say a good deal about The Hours, & my discov-
> ery: how I dig out beautiful caves behind my characters;
> I think that gives exactly what I want: humanity, humour,
> depth. The idea is that the caves shall connect, & each
> comes to daylight at the present moment.[8]

As usual, when she was working on a new novel, it was issues of form which most concerned her. And she had set
herself a challenging task for this modern novel: to write
the story of an unremarkable woman in London, to link
together two utterly different postwar lives with no apparent connection, and to set as she put it, "the world seen by
the sane and the insane side by side."[9] In a deliberate allusion to Joyce's *Ulysses* (which Woolf disliked, but had read
at least parts of with care and concentration), the novel
takes place on a single day. On this day, a middle-aged,
unemployed, married, wealthy, upper-class woman who
has just recovered from an illness has an unexpected re-
union with the man who wanted to marry her, and gives a
party; a young married man of a lower class, who has
fought in the war and is suffering from dementia, sees his
doctors, and kills himself. The narrative weaves between
the two without their ever meeting. The day's progress is
marked by the striking and chiming of bells which sometimes seem to relate to or to embody the characters.
(Hence the working title, "The Hours.") A variety of

strategies are used—repeated images, quotations, lines shared between characters, recurring memories—to link the two main stories and to bind the characters' separate lives into a whole shape. Like Proust's long novel, *À la recherche du temps perdu* (which she admired), also much concerned with memory and time, it culminates in the giving of a party, at which the hostess hears the news of the young man's death, and some sense of conclusion is reached, even though the party is itself (as in Proust) a disappointment. As the hours go past and the story of the day unfolds, the characters continually go down into the "caves" of their interior selves through memory, association, contemplation, vision, hallucination. A fluid, flexible narrative weaves between inner and outer time, immediate and imagined experiences, spaces, places, and minds.

"Character" is as important to her as form. All Woolf's essays on modern fiction, written mostly in the years leading up to *Mrs Dalloway*, are about what new tools can be used by the "modern" fiction writer to create character. She sees fiction as a form of life-writing. But she is at pains not to write autobiographical fiction, though many of her own emotions and experiences (including her breakdowns) are used for Clarissa Dalloway and Septimus Smith (and other characters in the novel, especially Clarissa's returning lover, Peter Walsh, who feels a stranger to England and its establishment world). Clarissa Dalloway, a rather superficial, charming, poorly read, apolitical, conservative woman in her early fifties, with a teenage daughter and a smart house in Westminster, is nothing like Virginia Woolf, though she shares her intense memories of childhood, her sexual ambivalence and withdrawal (her strongest erotic emotions have been for her girlhood friend, Sally Seton), her need for both solitude and society, and her preoccupation with illness and mortality combined with a passionate love of the life of the city. Her interior life is at odds with the conventional establishment figure who is seen on the surface. We are made aware of this inner life (via the novel's "tunnelling" methods) as Mrs Dalloway does the ordinary things a woman of her class and time would do—buying flowers, crossing the road, reading a message by the telephone pad, changing her clothes, mending her dress, getting ready for her party: the female domestic "trivia" that, in *A Room of One's Own*, Woolf would wryly argue has been thought less "important" as material for fiction than male subjects such as waging war or playing football.

Clarissa Dalloway has a vivid, strong, eager love of life, which has nothing to do with religious faith, but connects to her mystical sense of a form of immortality through memory and places. She detests coercion or bullying, those who want to force your soul or impose belief or obedience. This applies to the "love and religion" of Doris Kilman, her daughter's companion, of whom she is scornful and jealous; the psychiatric methods of the mental doctor, Sir William Bradshaw, a guest at her party; and the demanding, infantile love once offered by Peter Walsh. She seems edge on to the world she observes. This links her to the novel's other main character, Septimus.

"This late age of the world's experience had bred in them all a world of tears."[10] Septimus, himself dry-eyed, is the victim of "this late age of the world's experience." An estate agent's clerk in his twenties, married to an Italian girl who makes hats, he went to war in 1914 and fought through till 1918, and saw his best friend, Evans, killed. Septimus comes back from the war suffering from shell-shock. He can't feel anything; he is hallucinating visions of the dead and has paranoid delusions that messages are being sent to him for him to broadcast. He feels he is in total isolation and cannot communicate. (So he could stand as an extreme version of the experimental, misunderstood artist.) He is threatening to kill himself, and the doctors are on to him. His single story embodies all the terrible deaths and losses of the Great War that underlie the surface of the novel.

Septimus, far out on the edge of the normal world, violently enacts the social critique which Woolf wanted her novel to contain. His presence exposes the social complacency, the class divisions, hypocrisy, and exclusions of conservative postwar England—all sharply caricatured in the novel. These seem to crumble away in the light of Septimus's apocalyptic visions, triggered by the traumatic force of what he has witnessed in the trenches. Through the shimmer and glitter of 1920s partygoing London pushes up all that terror, despair, and grief.

Septimus's dementia, and its treatment, link him to Clarissa through the figure of Sir William Bradshaw, the eugenicist incarcerator of the mentally ill, who makes a tidy profit from his patients. When Sir William appears at Clarissa's party and mentions the suicide of one of his patients, Clarissa feels an inexplicable empathy. She perceives Septimus Smith's death as an act of free choice, as well as a thing of horror. In a sense he does it for her. The original plan for the novel was that she was "to kill herself, or perhaps merely to die at the end of the party."[11] (This is the authorial choice which will so interest Michael Cunningham.) Instead, Clarissa returns to her guests at the party, and is recognised as a living presence. The novel ends as if by claiming that it has achieved the job of fiction, of bringing her into being: "For there she was."

Mrs Dalloway is a "modern" novel in several senses. It's published in 1925, in the middle of the decade of the greatest experiments in modernist writing. It's contemporaneous: written between 1922 and 1924, it is set on a Wednesday in June 1923.[12] It treats difficult and challenging subjects—madness, shell-shock, suicide, bisexuality, sexual repression, maternal jealousy, and the catastrophic effects of war—in a suggestive, ironical, and unpolemical way. It makes bold experiments with a fictional form. It tells a whole history of a class and a society, even a country, on the basis of a single "day in a life"—not the methods of a Victorian or Edwardian novel. And it uses the "present moment" in the life of an ordinary woman, defined only by her married status and her surname in the title, as the centre for its meditation on life and death.

What does Michael Cunningham do with this contradiction in terms, a modernist classic, in his novel *The Hours*? First, and boldly, he sets it in America. Although Woolf never crossed the Atlantic, she once wrote a surreal, fascinated fantasy called "America Which I Have Never Seen," and might well have made the journey, after the war, if she had lived. It was a brilliant stroke to move the story of *Mrs Dalloway* from London to New York, with all the excitement of city life transferred to the streets of

Manhattan. Woolf's pleasure in "the bellow and the uproar . . . the triumph and the jingle" of "life; London; this moment of June" becomes Cunningham's stirring New York, "the roil and shock of it," its "racket" and "intricacy." Cunningham sees that *Mrs Dalloway* is a book in love with a city. It was written during the time that the Woolfs moved, in early 1924, into Bloomsbury from Richmond, the quiet suburb where they had been living since 1913 because of Virginia Woolf's breakdown and illness. London means life, the suburbs a living death. The city is where the party is going on. She wrote rejoicingly in her diary: "the whole of London . . . music, talk, friendship, city views, books, publishing, something central & inexplicable, all this is now within my reach, as it hasn't been since August 1913."[13]

Woolf's novel begins: "Mrs Dalloway said she would buy the flowers herself." Cunningham's novel begins twice, once with Woolf's suicide, and once with Mrs Dalloway setting out to buy flowers. But in this case "Mrs Dalloway" is a nickname given to a bisexual New Yorker, Clarissa Vaughan, by her friend and one-time lover, the writer Richard Brown, who is terminally ill with AIDS, at the end of the twentieth century. This Clarissa is fifty-two, like her namesake, but unlike her she is not married to Richard Dalloway; she lives with a woman called Sally, named after *Mrs Dalloway*'s Sally Seton. Like the original Mrs. Dalloway, she is giving a party—a party for her dying friend, to celebrate his winning a literary prize for his novel, whose subject is a woman who commits suicide.

There are two other narratives in *The Hours*. One is the story of a suburban American housewife, Laura

Brown, pregnant with her second child, who lives with her obtuse husband, just back from the war, and her anxious, overdependent little boy, in a Los Angeles suburb, in 1949. Like *Mrs Dalloway*, this is a postwar story. (In a last twist in the novel, the little boy turns out to be the future writer Richard Brown.) She is sleepwalking through her ordinary life which, on this day, consists in trying to make a cake for her husband's birthday party. But she is fighting against a strong sense of unreality, worthlessness, and longing for death. And she is reading *Mrs Dalloway*. (The critic Michael Wood, in his review of *The Hours*, observed that the chief difference between *Mrs Dalloway* and *The Hours* is that "no one in the first novel can have read the second, whereas almost everyone in the second seems to have read the first").[14] The fragile life of Laura Brown, trying to be a normal American wife and mother, is, I think, the most touching section of the book. We are left wondering to the end of the book whether, like the woman in her son's novel, she kills herself.

Cunningham's third story is that of Virginia Woolf, who is living in Richmond, married to Leonard, having her sister and her sister's children to a teaparty in June 1923—and writing *Mrs Dalloway*. She argues with her servants, is longing to move to London, feels jealous of her sister's family life, and is making her mind up whether or not to have Clarissa kill herself. In the end, she decides that "sane Clarissa will go on, loving London, loving her life of ordinary pleasures, and someone else, a deranged poet, a visionary, will be the one to die."[15] Framing that day in her life is the day of her suicide on 28 March 1941.

Cunningham's inventive, absorbing novel makes a sensitive reinvention of Woolf's inner life. He has a strong idea of what made Woolf's life heroic, of her dedication to her work in the teeth of illness, and her violent swings between moods of pleasure in life and abysses of depression. My reservations about his reimagining of Woolf stem from a biographer's squeamish reluctance to see a real person made over into a fictional character, with made-up thoughts and speeches. I found it hard to accept the tone of voice of a Virginia Woolf who thinks to herself, "Bless you, Quentin," or says to her husband, "If you send Nelly in to interrupt me I won't be responsible for my actions." In these invented scenes and conversations, the class details don't always ring quite true. I can't hear Virginia Woolf wanting to rush and "fix her hair," or Vanessa Bell commenting on "a lovely coat for Angelica at Harrods."[16] (Angelica would be much more likely to be wearing a cut-down jacket of Duncan Grant's, or a velvet cloak made out of old curtains.) But fiction, of course, is allowed to do this.

In the other two narratives, Woolfian echoes and parallels are woven in and out of Cunningham's American characters. Clarissa Vaughan's daughter Julia is, like Elizabeth Dalloway, in thrall to a woman who loathes Clarissa and makes her feel jealous. But this Doris Kilman is a militant feminist who resents Clarissa Vaughan's old-fashioned, bourgeois, domestic lesbianism. (This strand was cut in the film.) Septimus's hallucinations are re-enacted in Richard Brown's terminal illness: shell-shock and the traumatic aftermath of the Great War are translated into the trauma of the AIDS epidemic and its effect on individuals. Woolf's own struggle against

suicidal depression colours the story of Laura Brown.
(Mrs. Brown is the name Woolf gives, in her essay
"Mr Bennett and Mrs Brown," to the ordinary woman
who sets a challenge to all novelists.) Clarissa Vaughan,
like Clarissa Dalloway, is visited by an old friend, Louis,
a past lover of Richard's, while she is getting ready for
her party, an emotional visit in which he breaks down
and weeps. More playfully, the lunch with a Mayfair
hostess from which Mrs. Dalloway feels excluded in
Woolf's novel is turned into a lunch with a famous gay
actor, nudgingly called Oliver St. Ives. Royalty glimpsed
in Bond Street by Mrs. Dalloway becomes a film star—
perhaps Meryl Streep?—spotted on the streets of
Manhattan. (And, in the movie, there she is!)

Cunningham splits his story into three, Woolf splits
her story into two: both strategies raise the question of
how individual lives can connect to each other, and
whether a single person has more than one self, one way
of being. He is particularly interested in life as being,
like writing, a kind of performance. Cunningham's
Woolf pauses at the door of Hogarth House to pull herself together. "She had learned over the years that sanity
involves a certain measure of impersonation. . . . She is
the author; Leonard, Nelly, Ralph, and the others are the
readers."[17] Cunningham imagines Woolf impersonating
an identity for the benefit of onlookers and "readers,"
just as he is impersonating Woolf. He follows her interest, too, in the interior lives of ordinary women like
"Mrs Brown," and in the androgyneity of authorship
(here is a homosexual male writer impersonating a bisexual woman writer and writing about the lives of lesbians
and homosexuals). Like Woolf, he is asking questions

about how we value our lives. What is the value of "a life of ordinary pleasures"?[18] Can a few outstanding moments provide consolation against the long beat of the hours? Do writing—and reading—make life bearable? Cunningham derives from Woolf, too, an idea of immortality which has nothing to do with religion. Clarissa Dalloway imagines that "somehow in the streets of London, on the ebb and flow of things, she survived, Peter survived, lived in each other, she being part, she was positive, of the trees at home . . . part of people she had never met; being laid out like a mist between the people she knew best . . . but it spread ever so far, her life, herself." Cunningham imagines Woolf, after her death, in the river, still a part of "people she had never met": "All this enters the bridge, resounds through its wood and stone, and enters Virginia's body. Her face, pressed sideways to the piling, absorbs it all: the truck and the soldiers, the mother and the child."[19]

The Hours is not an imitation, or a pastiche, or exactly a rewriting; in fact this genre of book is hard to define. Michael Wood says that "*The Hours* is haunted by *Mrs Dalloway*. . . . The relationship between the two novels goes beyond allusion, and even beyond the modernist habit of borrowing previous literary structures which T. S. Eliot called 'the mythical method.'" The critic Seymour Chatman, in a piece called "*Mrs Dalloway*'s Progeny: *The Hours* as Second-Degree Narrative," refers to Gerard Genette's *Palimpsests* in an attempt to define this brand of intertextuality. Is it a sequel, a variation on a theme, a pastiche, a parallel, an imitation, a rewriting, a plagiarism, a caricature, an homage, or a transposition? Chatman argues that *The Hours* is "an alternative version of *Mrs Dalloway*" in which the main project is to present the "ordinariness" of gay life, to "demonstrate that the gay world is not exotic, but populated by ordinary people." His critique of *The Hours*, which he calls a "post-closet re-orientation," is that it "excludes the rest of the world": its interest in gender politics downplays or sidesteps the wider social politics of its original.[20]

The rewriting of Woolf's life and work takes a different shape again in the translation of *The Hours* from novel into screenplay and film. If an uncertainty of social register, a narrowing of political focus to issues of gender, and a simplifying dramatisation of Woolf's creative processes were the weaknesses of Cunningham's otherwise persuasive and attractive novel, the film of *The Hours*—if treated as a biopic—is much more vulnerable to charges of vulgarisation, inaccuracy, and sentimentalisation. Certainly its presentation of the social details of the Woolfs' lives was an irritant to this biographer. Hogarth House and Monk's House look too grand and elegant, more like Edith Wharton or Vita Sackville-West's house and garden than bohemian, messy, colourful Bloomsbury. The servants, in their matching uniforms, are too smartly turned out (though their ongoing battle with their difficult mistress is well done), and Vanessa, in a fine spiteful performance by Miranda Richardson, is absurdly posh, a high-society lady one couldn't possibly imagine picking up a paintbrush.

As for The Nose, Nicole Kidman, even with prosthetic addition and fixed scowl, doesn't look very like Virginia Woolf. She looks like Nicole Kidman wearing a nose.[21] She appears too young for the mid-forties author of *Mrs Dalloway*, let alone for the fifty-nine-year-old who kills herself. And she lacks charm. I wish something of Woolf's gleeful comedy, her hooting laughter, her allure, and her excited responses to people and gossip, had been caught. (It's a mark of Kidman's talent as an actress that those possibilities were so severely excluded: she could presumably have done all that if she'd been allowed to.)

David Hare's screenplay is more polemical than Michael Cunningham's novel. He makes much more of Woolf's rage with her doctors, and of the right to choose and proclaim one's sexuality. The three kisses that take place between women in film and novel—between Virginia and Vanessa, Laura Brown and her sick neighbour, Clarissa and her partner—are more deliberately emphasised than by Cunningham, who treats bisexuality as the normal condition of life. Everything is emphatic here. Virginia and Leonard (played with wonderful nervy intelligence by Stephen Dillane) hurl personal testimonies at each other on Richmond Station: "Only I can understand my own condition!" "It was done out of love!" (Virginia's outburst in this scene—"If I have to choose between Richmond and death, then I choose death!"—played rather differently in the Richmond Odeon than anywhere else in Britain.) In a big scene for Meryl Streep, it is Clarissa Vaughan, not, as in the novel, the old friend who is visiting her, who breaks down in hysterical tears while she is getting ready for her party. This sentimental expressiveness is in strong contrast to Woolf's own fiction, one of whose most striking and alarming qualities is its inhibition. All the women in the film are on the edge of breakdown; all of the emotional life is raging away on the surface (not, as in *Mrs Dalloway*, breaking through convention and guardedness). The acting and direction play up feelings for all they are worth. There are a great many scenes with long, emotional looks, tear-filled eyes, forgiving hugs, and expressions of love. (It's refreshing to have a caustic cameo performance in the New York flower shop from Eileen Atkins, more usually seen as Virginia Woolf.)

For all its polemical earnestness about the mistreatment of mental illness and the constrictions imposed on Virginia Woolf after her breakdown, the film evacuates her life of political intelligence or social acumen, returning her to the position of doomed, fey, mad victim. I wish, for instance, that she could have been seen setting type at the Press alongside Leonard, as she so often did, instead of wandering off for gloomily creative walks on Richmond Hill. I wish that the idea of "creativity" didn't consist in an inspirational flash, of the first sentence leaping to the novelist's mind, shortly followed by a whole book. (Woolf took about three years, drafting and redrafting, to write *Mrs Dalloway*, and the first sentence she started with wasn't the first sentence she ended up with.) I wish that to the inattentive viewer it didn't look as if Virginia Woolf committed suicide just after finishing *Mrs Dalloway*. (Sure enough, one short review of the film, on a website called filmcritic.com, read: "Mentally ill author Virginia Woolf (Nicole Kidman) is on suicide watch in 1920s England as she pens her novel *Mrs Dalloway*.")[22] Above all, I wish her suicide hadn't been transformed into a picturesque idyll. Woolf was no Ophelia: she drowned herself on a cold day in March in a dangerous, ugly river where the water runs so fast that nothing grows on the bare banks. She was wearing an old fur coat, wellington boots, and a hat held on by an elastic band. Whether she jumped or walked, dropped under or struggled, we don't know. When I challenged Stephen Daldry in an interview about his version of the suicide, he responded: "We only had Kidman for four weeks in June, and we couldn't exactly strip the trees."[23]

Where novel and film come together in an impressive tribute to Virginia Woolf, however, is in their eloquence about a subject which, so many years after *Mrs Dalloway*, and the death of its author, is still a highly problematic one. Can we choose whether to live or die? "It is possible to die. . . . She—or anyone—could make a choice like that. It is a reckless, vertiginous thought," Laura Brown thinks in the novel.[24] In all three narratives, a decision is being made about suicide. Why must someone die in her novel, Leonard Woolf asks Virginia, in the film. "Someone has to die in order that the rest of us should value life more," she replies. Laura Brown puts the "vertiginous thought" behind her, and goes home, at least this time, to her family. Richard Brown, before he slides out of his top-floor window, tells Clarissa that he has stayed alive for her, but now she must let him go. How should we treat death? David Hare—perhaps too consolingly— imagines the voice of Virginia Woolf telling us, as she leaves us, that she has mastered this question, and understands what to do: "to look life in the face and to know it for what it is; to love it for what it is, and then to put it away."

The film of *The Hours* gained enormous publicity and won some prizes; and it sent readers back in droves, not only to Cunningham's novel but also to *Mrs Dalloway*, which for a short time became the number one paperback on Amazon's sales list, the first time the book had ever been a bestseller. There was even a poem called "The Hours" written about the making of the film, by Mark Doty, who watched the filming of Clarissa going to buy flowers in a corner of New York sprayed with artifical snow. (One of the licences the film took was to set the Mrs Dalloway story in winter, not in June.)

> Clarissa
> buying the flowers herself.
> I take it personally. As if,
>
> no matter what, this emblem persists:
> a woman went to buy flowers, years ago,
> in a novel, and was entered
>
> by the world . . .
> . . . .
> Though they continue, shadow and replica,
> copy and replay—adapted, reduced,
> reframed—beautiful versions—a paper cone of asters,
> golden dog nipping at a glove—fleeting,
>
> and no more false than they are true.[25]

"No more false than they are true" would have been a useful line for some angry Woolfians, who were "taking it personally," to bear in mind. *The Hours*, though a popular and widely enjoyed film, created considerable dismay in some circles. As always with Woolf's posthumous reputation, there were transatlantic differences. In Britain, the film brought Woolf's usual critics out from under their stones; the novelist Philip Hensher, always a vindictively anti-Woolfian voice, wrote a piece called "Virginia Woolf Makes Me Want to Vomit," taking the opportunity to attack her "truly terrible novels . . . inept, ugly, fatuous, badly written and revoltingly self-indulgent."[26] Some good fun was had at the expense of The Nose. (One critic suggesting that in the scene where Virginia lays her head down on the grass next to the dead bird which her niece has left in the garden for burial, she is comparing beaks.) In America, the film was mocked by some reviewers for pretentiousness and liberal pieties: for instance as "a preposterous faux-feminist manifesto that blames the woes of the modern day female on her historical disconnectedness." It also came under attack (Daldry told me in interview) from spokesmen for Catholic churches calling it "an abomination" which "should be banned. . . . There have been demonstrations outside cinemas, and suggestions that we're celebrating women who've abandoned their children."[27]

Readers and viewers more sympathetic to feminism, gay culture and Woolf had other kinds of criticism (though the film had plenty of admirers, too). The family, in the voice of Vanessa Bell's granddaughter Virginia Nicholson, complained bitterly about Kidman's inappropriateness in the part, her gloom and lack of humour, and, particularly, about the absurd representation of Vanessa. But, as Nicholson admitted: "How can I possibly look at the film objectively? From my angle, whatever they do is going to be wrong." In a letter to me, she added sadly: "This film will inform the perceptions of Virginia Woolf of a generation of cinema-goers."[28]

Many Woolfians were no happier. Chat rooms and Woolf e-mail sites resounded with criticisms of the film.

Here are two characteristic examples of the arguments, one more hostile than the other. The first is by Roberta Rubenstein, the second by Maria Alvarez:

> Like a copy of a copy, Woolf is diminished through replication. . . . Woolf is revealed . . . as a very serious, rather abstracted woman whose mind wanders from the details at hand to the details of the novel she's writing, who argues with servants, who causes her husband distress, who commits suicide by drowning. I'm afraid that too many film-goers will take from *The Hours* the impression of nothing more than a sad, eccentric writer—a figure far simpler than the intellectually robust and emotionally complex Virginia Woolf. . . . I'm afraid for the real Woolf. I'm concerned that she has been made into Virginia Woolf lite.[29]

> Woolf was a protean creature. . . . *The Hours* sympathetically perpetuates one stereotype of Woolf—the restless, tortured, "mad" artist in enforced exile from real life, and ultimately torn apart by this alienation. [But the film] will ensure that a new generation of young women will reinvent and reappraise her.[30]

These sorts of views were rounded up in a piece by Patricia Cohen in the *New York Times* for 15 February 2003, titled "The Nose Was the Final Straw." (The theme of the piece was trailed: "A witty writer and activist has become a loser with an absurd proboscis, her devotees say.")[31] Cohen commented: "Many Woolfians are fuming, arguing that their idol has been turned into a pathetic, suicide-obsessed creature, her politics ignored, her personality distorted, and even her kisses inaccurately portrayed."

Various well-known American Woolf scholars were cited, Jane Marcus dismissing the novel (as well as the film) as "a tiny, insignificant spin-off from a great book," Brenda Silver advising, "If you want to read Virginia Woolf, then read Virginia Woolf." A Woolf doctoral student said, "What really put me off was the Nose", and added bemusedly: "Were Woolf's contemporaries obsessed with her nose?" The Vice-President of the International Virginia Woolf Society, Vara Neverow, exclaimed: "Oh my God, did they have to drown her twice?" And she spoke of "having to defend my territory." Michael Cunningham, writing to me about this debate, asked: "How dare she, how dare anyone, consider Woolf his or her 'territory'? I know of no other figure who inspires such ferocious possessiveness."[32]

At the Virginia Woolf Conference at Smith College in June 2003, where the tone was predominantly feminist and pro-Woolfian, a panel chaired by Brenda Silver discussed the issue of possessiveness. This was a conversation about the struggle between authority and ownership on the one hand, and "versioning," or "appropriation," or "translation," on the other. The film studies expert on the panel abandoned all notions of "fidelity" in favour of an interest in "transformation." The English feminist critic Michèle Barrett dwelt (like Seymour Chatman) on the shift in "political burden" from *Mrs Dalloway* to the film of *The Hours*. She had been irritated by David Hare's claim in his introduction to the published screenplay that the devastation of AIDS provided a parallel to the devastation of the First World War. Barrett argued that there was really no parallel, but that the "political centre or theme" of *Mrs Dalloway* had been dropped "in favour of a different political scene, a meditation on the implications of sexual choice." Daniel Mendelsohn, who had written a thoughtful piece on the different "version-ings" of Woolf by Cunningham, Hare, and Daldry, in the *New York Review of Books*, argued that it is impossible not to think about "a literary figure whom we all know" in relation to the film's version of her, impossible not to ask "well, precisely *what* does this woman with this funny nose have to do with Virginia Woolf?" His reaction to the film was that it "flattened her out," and "re-inscribed the popular clichè about female creators, that they walk around glowering all the time." He minded that "there are now fifty million American cinema-goers who think of Virginia Woolf as that dame who drowned herself and wore brown clothes."[33] All agreed, more or less, that the film of *The Hours* was a kind of "biopic," which had made up a version of Virginia Woolf's life-story.

Does it matter if the film's version of Virginia Woolf pre-vails for a time? There is no one answer. Yes, because it distorts and to a degree misrepresents her, and for any form of re-creation, of any significant life, in any medium, there is a responsibility to accuracy. No, be-cause she continues to be reinvented—made up, and made over—with every new adapter, reader, editor, critic, and biographer. There is no owning her, or the facts of her life. The Nose is her latest and most popular incar-nation, but she won't stay fixed under it for ever. At the end of *Orlando*, Woolf's teasing spoof on conventional biography, her hero/heroine, reaching the present day, sniffing its smells and powdering her nose, calls all her various selves together. For "a biography is considered complete if it merely accounts for six or seven selves, whereas a person may well have as many thousand." James Ramsay realises, as he finally gets close "to the lighthouse,"[34] and finds it isn't a bit like he expected it to be, that "nothing was simply one thing."

Chapter 3

···

Jane Austen Faints

Jane Austen's novels are kinds of life-writing, much concerned with family plots, gossip, stories, guesswork, knowledge, assessments of human behaviour, and the importance of reading people right: their histories, their motives, their secrets and desires. There's an intriguing demonstration of this in the scenes between Anne Elliot and Mrs. Smith in Austen's last finished novel, *Persuasion*. These scenes have been criticised for awkwardness and clumsy plotting, and it's assumed she would have revised them if she had not fallen ill. But the rough edges of an author's work can be very revealing, especially an author usually as polished and meticulous as this one.

The situation is this. Mrs. Smith, once Miss Hamilton, was kind to Anne when, aged fourteen, she went "unhappy to school" after her mother's death. But she is now, twelve years later, an impoverished widow, crippled with rheumatism, living in confined lodgings in Bath. Anne visits her (much to the scorn of her snobbish father, Sir Walter the baronet) and admires Mrs. Smith's capacity for making so much of the diminished thing that her life is. Mrs. Smith tells Anne about her landlady's sister, Nurse Rooke, who visits Mrs. Smith and reports to her something of what's going on in the town.

Mrs. Smith says of this offstage character: "Hers is a line for seeing human nature. . . . She is sure to have something to relate that is entertaining and profitable, something that makes one know one's species better. One likes to hear what is going on." Anne observes that she must have many sickroom stories of heroism and fortitude; Mrs. Smith looks doubtful, and says that they are more often stories of weakness, "selfishness and impatience." This "line for seeing human nature," then, is realistic and uncensored.

It turns out, in the second long scene between Anne and Mrs. Smith, that Mrs. Smith also gets her local information from "a laundress and a waiter." Through her sources, Mrs. Smith has heard a rumour that Anne is likely to be soon engaged to her cousin, Mr. Elliot. Only when Anne disabuses her of this idea does Mrs. Smith expose to her Mr. Elliot's "real" character; he is a heartless, designing, "wary cold blooded being," set on advancing himself financially and socially through marriage, and plotting to inherit the baronetcy through marrying Anne. As proof of this, Mrs. Smith shows Anne a ten-year-old letter, dated 1803, which is very rude about Anne's father. Anne is shocked by this, but also feels that she shouldn't be reading "private correspondence." Mrs. Smith explains how she has heard about Mr. Elliot's plots via Nurse Rooke—whom she calls "my historian"—who has got it from the wife of a Colonel Wallis, who is Mr. Elliot's friend. "The stream is as good as at first; the little rubbish it collects in the turnings, is easily moved away." Once Anne accepts this "representation of Mr. Elliot," Mrs. Smith provides even more dramatic evidence of his past villainy: he was responsible for ruining Mrs. Smith's late husband, and she has letters to prove it.

Awkwardly as this slab of information is bumped into the novel, it makes a vivid version of biography. Following the trail of the story and clearing away the rubbish that's accrued to it through gossip and rumour, using written evidence to prove a point, drawing on whatever sources of information you can get, building up a "representation" of the character: these are the biographer's jobs. These scenes invoke, too, the moral reservations so often attached to biography—dislike of gossip, distrust of "low" sources of information, squeamishness about reading private correspondence, suspecting witnesses of having a private agenda. So the "Mrs. Smith" episode in *Persuasion* makes a good entry point for some thoughts about the telling of Jane Austen's life-story, which has had to negotiate a number of "turnings" in the stream and a fair amount of accumulated "rubbish."[1]

The best-known fact about Jane Austen's posthumous life is that her story was guarded and shaped by her family. The legacy of that guardianship is seen on the covers of the last six biographies of Jane Austen, published between 1984 and 2001: they all have the same picture of her, because that's the only one there is: Cassandra Austen's 1811 pen and watercolour drawing of her sister, with the cap, the curls, the beady brown eyes, the crossed arms, and the wry (even "caustic") sideways look. It is the only front-face portrait of Jane Austen (the original image was touched up and prettified for the family memoir) and it's a symbol of how, for many years, the family kept control of her image. As Marilyn Butler put it in a review of some of those recent biographies, "for

the first century at least [after her death], the main quali-
fication for the task [of being Jane Austen's biographer]
was to be a relative."[2]

First there was her brother Henry Austen's "Biographical Notice," published in the posthumous 1818 edition
of *Northanger Abbey* and *Persuasion*. Then there was her
niece Anna Lefroy's "Recollections of Aunt Jane" of
1864, and her other niece Caroline Austen's memoir
("My Aunt Jane Austen") of 1867, unpublished until
1952 (followed by her "Reminiscences," written in the
1870s). Then there was her nephew James Edward
Austen-Leigh's *A Memoir of Jane Austen*, of 1870, and
her great-niece (daughter of her niece Anna) Fanny
Lefroy's "Family History," from the 1880s. Then there
was the 1884 selection of her letters by Lord Brabourne,
son of Austen's niece Fanny Knight, carelessly edited,
with an effusive commentary, and dedicated to Queen
Victoria. Early in the twentieth century, there was her
great-nephew and great-great-nephew William and
Richard Austen-Leigh's *The Life and Letters: A Family
Record*, of 1913, on which the Austen scholar and editor
Deirdre Le Faye would base her *Jane Austen: A Family
Record*, first published in 1989 and revised in 2004. These
family versions are revealingly compared by Kathryn
Sutherland in her 2002 edition of some of these mem-
oirs, in which she notes that there are rival claims, within
them, to "the more authentic portrait" of Jane Austen.[3]

Deirdre Le Faye edited a fine new collection of Jane
Austen's letters in 1995. But one feature of the family's
lingering control over Austen's body of work is that nu-
merous letters, or parts of letters—the sort of evidence

Mrs. Smith was able to flourish in front of Anne Elliot—were destroyed by Cassandra. Austen's sister obliterated the evidence of her responses to the crucial events in her life, such as the sudden death of Cassandra's fiancé in 1797, the family's move from Steventon, and Austen's possible romantic involvements. It's long been argued that the effect of this "culling" of Cassandra's is, as one of Austen's biographers, Claire Tomalin, puts it, to leave the impression that "her sister was dedicated to trivia. The letters rattle on, sometimes almost like a comedian's patter. Not much feeling, warmth or sorrow has been allowed through. . . . You have to keep reminding yourself how little they represent of her real life, how much they are an edited and contrived version." A more recent counterargument is that the letters, rather than being disparaged by comparison with the novels, should be attended to for what they do reveal, and for the "texture of domestic life" they present. Or, perhaps, as Sutherland suggests, there "was never a confiding correspondence to hold back": it's just that biographers are suspicious of "gaps and silences."[4]

Apart from the letters, most of the evidence biographers have to draw on is family anecdote and memoir, some written long after the event. If only Austen had kept a journal, as Mr. Tilney in *Northanger Abbey* assumes Catherine Morland must certainly do, like all other young ladies of her class! Instead of which, her biographers have had to make do with stories and legends handed down and repeated: certainly a muddied stream. Take the mysterious story of Jane Austen's failed romance with a handsome clergyman in Devonshire. This hazy episode is the only candidate for a serious love affair, apart from her flirtation, at twenty, with Tom Lefroy, which was put an end to by family pressures. It's a family legend which originated in a remark said to have been made by Cassandra.

> There is a family tradition that during one of these seaside holidays between 1801 and 1804 Jane met the only man whom she could seriously have wished to marry, had fortune been kinder to her. Cassandra knew the details of this brief episode, but in her later life passed on to her niece Caroline Austen merely the barest outline of what had happened years before. In 1870 Caroline wrote out the account, for her brother's use in preparing the second edition of the *Memoir*.[5]

Caroline's story was that her Aunt Cassandra (whose own fiancé had died tragically when she was twenty-four), on meeting a good-looking man in 1828, said he reminded her of the clergyman in Devonshire who was "greatly attracted" by Caroline's Aunt Jane, and who said he would come back to see her. But news then followed that he had died. Deirdre Le Faye comments that "in the absence of any further evidence from outside sources . . . Jane's stillborn romance can only remain 'nameless and dateless.' " But the very fact that the story was so hazy attracted biographers to it. One Austen devotee, Constance Pilgrim, even made up a whole book about the romance, *Dear Jane: A Biographical Study*. Joan Rees, in *Jane Austen: Woman and Writer* (1976), wrote: "According to family tradition . . . Jane Austen fell deeply in love *more or less at first sight* [my italics] with an extremely charming young clergyman who has never been satisfactorily identified.

Although he returned her feelings . . . [she] received the tragic news that, just like Cassandra's fiancé, the man she loved had suddenly died." Rees continues: "*What is hard to doubt* [my italics] is that she had been able to draw on experience as well as imagination for her descriptions of the states of falling and being in love." The biographer John Halperin, following this line, exclaims, with no provisos: "This time she had *loved*! [his italics]." The legend satisfies conventional habits of explaining the life of a spinster or old maid as one of thwarted love; and it provides ammunition for romantic readings (as in the film *Shakespeare in Love*) which want to link a personal experience of lifelong, hopeless longing with the plots of the novels, so that Fanny Price or Anne Elliot can be read as standing in for a lovelorn Jane Austen. But the legend of thwarted love can also fuel a negative view of a resentful, bitter, caustic Jane Austen, which reads her irony as "pathological, a problem any good husband could relieve. . . . All social criticism written by women is born of disappointment in love." More recent biographies have chosen to dismiss the mysterious Devonshire clergyman as an invention of Cassandra's or as "mistily romantic" as the Devon coast itself.[6]

In the matter of the lost clergyman, biographers are responding, according to their different agendas, to the family's construction—a very successful one—of a version of Jane Austen which held sway for many years. In Marilyn Butler's words, this was "that the author was a very domestic woman, and that outside her family she had no profound attachments or interests." "Immediately after Jane Austen's death," notes the novelist Carol Shields in her sympathetic short life of Austen, "she was entombed in veneration." The Austen family's Jane Austen was not a professional writer, but a home-loving daughter, sister, and aunt, and above all a good Christian. Her gravestone inscription, prepared by her brothers, remarked on "the benevolence of her heart, the sweetness of her temperament, the extraordinary endowment of her mind," but did not mention her books. Her brother Henry's "Biographical Notice" of 1818 emphasised that she wrote with "no hope of fame nor profit" and that "in public she turned away from any allusion to the character of an authoress." Henry Austen drew attention to her "perfect placidity of temper," the kindness of her wit, her tranquillity, her complete lack of interest in fame and money, her reading of "moral" writers, and her being "thoroughly religious and devout." This has been well described as an attempt "to project an image of a ladylike, unmercenary, unprofessional, private, delicate, and domestic author."[7]

Though the 1870 *Memoir* by her nephew James Austen-Leigh gave a livelier impression, and allowed that Austen could be funny about her neighbours, her nephew (by then an elderly clergyman) was at pains to add that "she was as far as possible from being censorious or satirical." It's often been noted that Jane Austen was becoming "Victorianised," and the *Memoir* characterises her above all as a shining light in her own home—"a comfortable, approachable figure who put down her needlework to pick up her pen"—rather like a later Victorian heroine, Dickens's Esther Summerson, in *Bleak House*.

Underneath [Jane Austen's bright qualities, writes James Austen-Leigh] lay the strong foundations of sound sense

and judgment, rectitude of principle, and delicacy of feeling, qualifying her equally to advise, assist, or amuse. She
was, in fact, as ready to comfort the unhappy, or to nurse
the sick, as she was to laugh and jest with the light-
hearted. . . . [Her nieces] know what a sympathising friend
and judicious adviser they found her to be in the many little difficulties and doubts of early womanhood. . . .

She was a humble, believing Christian. Her life had been
passed in the performance of home duties, and the cultiva-
tion of domestic affections, without any self-seeking or
craving after applause.

Whatever it was made her a writer seems quite separate
from the rest of her life:

Hers was a mind well balanced on a basis of good sense,
sweetened by an affectionate heart, and regulated by fixed
principles; so that she was to be distinguished from many
other amiable and sensible women only by that peculiar
genius which shines out clearly enough in her works, but
of which a biographer can make little use.

When illness struck her, she patiently readied herself for
death. Austen's illness has been variously diagnosed as
Bright's disease, Addison's disease, a lymphoma such as
Hodgkin's disease, or breast cancer; the 1870 memoir
does not go into unpleasant details. As with the fewness
of portraits or the haziness of love affairs, whatever had
most to do with her bodily life is hardest to track down.

One Victorian reviewer of the *Memoir* asked: "Might
not we . . . recognise her officially as 'dear Aunt Jane'?"
A recent feminist critic comments grimly: "We might
and we did."[8] The family story fed into versions of Jane

Austen which have been in contention for well over a hundred years. Austen studies—editing, criticism, biography, social history—are now as conflicted and oppositional as the original accounts of her were tranquil and benign. As Deidre Lynch—a critic who specialises in the Austen wars, with all their "passionate acrimony" and "vehemence of partisanship"—observes: "a customary method of establishing one's credentials as a reader of Austen has been to suggest that others simply will insist on liking her in inappropriate ways."[9] But the peculiarity of the Austen wars is that although the different versions of her can be seen to be very much of their time—a late-Victorian Jane Austen, a wartime Jane Austen, a post-sixties feminist Jane Austen—they don't supersede one another, but coexist and jostle for position. It's as though the body of this author—which her relatives tried so hard to sanctify—is continually being torn into parts and put back together again.

The family version lent itself easily to an "English Heritage" Jane Austen, benign heroine of an idyllic, rural, golden-age England, the saintly and serene maiden aunt making the most of her sheltered uneventful life, her wit and wisdom always on the side of morality, restraint, and good sense. This Tory Jane Austen, beloved of the Janeites and the Jane Austen Society, and cherished by nineteenth- and early twentieth-century admirers such as Kipling, Macaulay, and Lord David Cecil, has been ferociously attacked, but hasn't gone away. It gets into the Austen tourist industry and the hugely popular Jane Austen movies, even though rural England of the late eighteenth century has long ceased to be described by historians as the clean, green, pastoral of the nostalgic film adaptations, all bonnets and carriages and parks and starched pinnies, and Colin Firth and Alan Rickman striding about in ruffled shirts and shiny boots.

Recent critics and biographers are more likely to describe Austen's landscape and social context in terms of instability, exploitation, provincial discontent, rural crime, social climbing, and imperial profiteering, and the Austen family as, in Marilyn Butler's phrase, "a family of meritocrats struggling to get ahead in a competitive, money-driven society."[10] Ever since the psychologist D. W. Harding's crucial *Scrutiny* essay of 1940 on Austen's "regulated hatred," and the American critic Marvin Mudrick's 1952 book on her defensive use of irony, she has been read (by some) as expressing anger and resentment in her fiction against a life of constriction and repression.[11] That idea of a resentful double life, kept down by a family censorship in which Austen was herself complicit, has done a great deal to demolish the benign Jane Austen of the Janeites. So has a quite different, severe historical account of Austen (pioneered by Marilyn Butler in the 1970s), not as a secretly resentful misfit, but as a hard-line Tory purveyor of establishment values, summarised (by critics who disagree with Butler) as providing "arms for the bourgeois thought police" and endorsing "a repressive middle-class ideology of manners": "an anti-Jacobin novelist writing in defence of patriarchal authority and the country house which provided one of its most potent symbols."[12]

Yet the English Heritage Jane Austen still lives on, as in Nigel Nicolson's *The World of Jane Austen* ("she loved the luxury of Godmersham . . . above all she loved its countryside . . . where everyone seemed perennially at peace with each other and the external world"), or in the glossy pages of Susan Watkins's 1996 Thames & Hudson picture book *Jane Austen in Style*, the cover of which shows a grand country house in Kent, and, in an inset medallion, the dance scene, starring Jennifer Ehle, from the BBC film of *Pride and Prejudice*. Watkins's introduction promises that "in these pages, from the vantage point of a particular English country gentlewoman, a journey is made through the society and surroundings of a group of people of unsurpassed elegance and refinement." "Here we will see *how* the country gentry lived— in an ambience of cultural politeness, with a keen though delicate sensibility, well balanced by common sense." That's the long-established Jane Austen of the Janeites, purveying nostalgia for "a golden age of the English gentry." That version of Austen was at its peak in the early twentieth century, when "images of the late eighteenth century countryside . . . connoted a harmonious refuge from the modern world between 1918 and 1945." But the remarkable thing about the genteel, nostalgic, benign version of Austen is its persistence, not only in picture books but also in literary criticism. It creeps into, for instance, a critical book of 1987, which concludes that "in the poignancy of the secular situations she sets before us, and of the human inadequacies they reveal, we may find the angelic dismay, sorrow and compassion."[13]

Critics wanting to construct a more robust, less sanctified Austen have to push hard against the genteel, nostalgic version. At the same time that "Austenmania"— movies, coffee-table books and mugs, T-shirts, guided tours of Chawton—has vigorously persisted, there's an equally vigorous, ongoing proliferation of rival critical,

bibliographical, and historical readings.[14] Editors of her
work are starting to undo the received shape of the oeu-
vre, established by R. W. Chapman from the 1920s onwards in his editions of the novels, the letters, and the
"minor works." Feminist critics of Austen (Margaret
Kirkham, Mary Poovey, Nancy Armstrong, Claudia
Johnson) have for some time been questioning the "gendered public-private ascription of spheres of activity"
which commits Austen to the realm of domestic minu-
tiae and to a local, apolitical treatment of the "little bit
(two inches wide) of ivory," her much-quoted descrip-
tion of her own scope and materials. It has long been
argued that "Jane Austen was deeply involved in, and
cognisant of, the major ideological debates of her time."
One social historian looking at Austen in the context
of Regency England has argued with the persistence of
the "polite" version of Jane Austen which "still attempts
to deny that she ever wrote about fleas, naked cupids
and bad breath." A Marxist critic of her work, following
the example of Raymond Williams, claims that "far
from endorsing the given, and emergent values of late-
eighteenth-century capitalism she was in many ways
deeply critical of them." An influential feminist critic,
Terry Castle, dared to suggest in 1995 that Jane Austen's
closest and most passionate relationship was with her sister Cassandra ("Was Jane Austen Gay?") and was greeted
with a storm of abuse from Jane's devotees, as though
Castle had somehow "polluted the shrine." Postcolonial
critics of Austen, beginning with Edward Said in "Jane
Austen and Empire" in 1989, observe that, now that she
has been thoroughly politicised, studies of Austen involve an interrogation of the concept of "English" and of

the classical canon of English Literature. It's argued by such critics that Austen's function has been "as an entropic model of the backward look to the green core," and that she has stood in the canon of English literature as "the benign female signature of nostalgic agrarian Romanticism."[15]

Biography tends to lag behind critical debate, but these hotly contested readings of Jane Austen—many of which, like Terry Castle's, involve biographical disputes—have begun to make their way into the telling of Jane Austen's life-story. That story, and its versions, demonstrate very vividly the argument of the American feminist critic Carolyn Heilbrun, that, until recently, biographies of women who don't fit into the standard models have been difficult to write, and have been written "under the constraints of acceptable discussion." Even if the family version of Jane Austen's life is resisted or demolished, her story raises particular challenges for the biographer. Heilbrun noted (in 1988) that it was still difficult to find a way of writing about "the choices and pain of the women who did not make a man the centre of their lives."[16] If the virtuous and benign—or thwarted and bitter—maiden aunt is refused as the working model, what other shapes can this story take?

Since the 1960s, biographies of Austen have placed the emphasis on the frustrations of her familial position of dependency, her long servitude to her hypochondriacal mother, her cloistered relationship with Cassandra, the loneliness, even desperation, of her middle age, her realism and misanthropy. The gap between the pious self-effacement of the family version, and the mordant wit and energetic, worldly-wise brilliance of the novels, is frequently noted. And the idealised "dear Aunt Jane" is undermined by pointing to the notable eruptions of viciousness or grimness in the letters—notoriously on Mrs. Hall of Sherbourn who "was brought to bed yesterday of a dead child, some weeks before she expected, oweing to a fright.—I suppose she happened unawares to look at her husband."[17]

One of the most dramatic moments in the life, and one of the places where all of Austen's biographers have to decide what to do with the handed-down family versions, is the scene in which Jane Austen faints. The story is told, sticking closely to the family reports (and without much questioning of them), by Deirdre Le Faye, in *Jane Austen: A Family Record*. Le Faye's sources are Fanny Lefroy's unpublished Family History of the early 1880s (citing her mother Anna's report), a letter from Caroline Austen to James Edward Austen-Leigh of 1869 (which was reprinted in R. W. Chapman's *Jane Austen: Facts and Problems* in 1948), the 1870 *Memoir*, the 1913 *Life*, and the letters from Jane to Cassandra early in 1801.

Jane (as Le Faye calls her) had been away from home (the rectory at Steventon in Hampshire where she was born and had lived all her twenty-five years), staying at Ibthorpe with her friend Martha Lloyd (whose sister Mary was married to one Austen brother, James, and who would later marry another Austen brother, Frank). Cassandra was also away from home, staying at Godmersham Park in Kent, home of their distant cousins, the wealthy Knights, who had adopted Jane's brother Edward. (Any one moment in Austen's life immediately brings in such thick swathes of family connections.) The story, as pieced together by Le Faye, is as follows:

> While Jane was away, the latent strain of impetuosity in the Austens suddenly manifested itself in her father; and family tradition says that as she and Martha arrived from Ibthorpe early in December [1800] they were met in the rectory hall by Mrs Austen, who greeted them with: "Well, girls, it is all settled, we have decided to leave Steventon in such a week and go to Bath"—and to Jane the shock of this intelligence was so great that she fainted away. Mary Lloyd, who was also present to greet her sister, remembered that Jane was "greatly distressed."
>
> No letters to Cassandra survive for the month of December 1800, which suggests that she destroyed those in which Jane gave vent to feelings of grief and perhaps even resentment at being so suddenly uprooted from her childhood home without any prior consultation by her parents as to her own opinions in the matter—Cassandra too had presumably been left in ignorance of this decision. "My Aunt was very sorry to leave her native home, as I have heard my Mother relate" . . . To exchange permanently the homely but comfortable rectory and the fields and woodlands of Hampshire for a tall narrow terrace house in one of Bath's stone-paved streets must have been [a] dismaying . . . prospect to Jane. . . . So hasty, indeed, did Mr Austen's decision appear to the Leigh-Perrots [Austen's maternal uncle and his wife] that they suspected the reason to be a growing attachment between Jane and William Digweed, one of the four brothers at Steventon manor house. There is not the slightest evidence of this supposition in Jane's letters. . . . It seems most probable that Mr Austen's age

and Mrs Austen's continuing ill-health were the deciding
factors for retirement . . .

> By January 1801 Jane had recovered her composure,
> and the six letters written in the New Year are in her usual
> style of cheerful irony. . . . The plans for the retirement to
> Bath naturally figure largely in these letters: . . . "I get
> more & more reconciled to the idea of our removal. . . . It
> must not be generally known however that I am not sacri-
> ficing a great deal in quitting the Country—or I can ex-
> pect to inspire no tenderness, no interest in those we leave
> behind."[18]

Jane Austen's faint seems to provide a clue to many as-
pects of her life, and not surprisingly it has been a test
case for biographers. "Why," asks Kathryn Sutherland,
who looks closely at the family versions of this scene,
"does this one distressing moment matter, and why do
subsequent biographers embellish it so enthusiastically?"
It exposes her dependent position, as a woman of
twenty-five unable to make her own choices. It has implications for her relations with her mother, who could
be read, in this anecdote, as bludgeoning and insensitive.
It suggests the kind of quick, intense, and sensitive
responses which we may want to identify as a mark of
genius. It provides a rare sight of her emotions expressing themselves in a physical gesture. It may imply that
the habits of a rooted, settled life made the decision to
move a great shock. Beyond that, it makes us aware of
the family circle, especially women, who were her witnesses and interpreters, and of the difficulty of piecing
together the story from the gaps and silences in the letters and from the handed-down evidence. And it seems

to offer an intimate moment for biographers to make the most of, since—as John Wiltshire puts it, writing on biographers' desires to get close up to Jane Austen— "biography's appeal to readers is inseparable from the dream of possession of, and union with, the subject."[19]

The faint is a challenge for readers of Austen's life and works who see her as a rational, ironic, conservative, Johnsonian satirist.[20] Fainting, after all, is one of many symptoms of extreme, even alarming sensibility (or of affectation of sensibility) which Austen, if read as an ironist, was so concerned to satirise or regulate in her fiction. John Mullan, writing on "the language of feeling" in the eighteenth century, notes how women are represented as "inherently liable to internal disorder," and how feminine sensibility "exists on the edge of an abyss," where an extreme of sensibility becomes—as for Marianne Dashwood—"dangerous affliction." Fainting was one of the much-noted symptoms of such dangerous extremes of hysteria and hypochondria. Devotees who praise Austen for her Augustan wit and wisdom express some anxieties over the faint. The grand-daughter of the author of the *Memoir*, Emma Austen-Leigh, writing in 1939 on *Jane Austen in Bath*, thinks it was unlike her: "Tradition says Jane fainted away from the shock, and although this sensibility is not quite in keeping with what we know of her character, there is little doubt that for a time she was very unhappy." A leading academic "Janeite" of the early twentieth century, A. C. Bradley, takes a more gallant, protective tone (often used by her male admirers in this period), but also sees the faint as uncharacteristic: "We learn that, when suddenly told of her father's decision to leave Steventon, their home in

the country, and reside in Bath, she fainted away; a fact
which I mention with some compunctions, for she would
have been horrified by the idea that this proof of her
'sensibility' would some day be made public."[21] Note
that both of these apologists use the phrase "fainted
away," which they have taken from the 1913 *Life*, somehow more elegant and less brutal than "fainted."

That rational, controlled Jane Austen, who would
have been embarrassed by showing her sensibility in
public, has been countered by writers who have become
interested in the bodily life in her writings. John
Wiltshire's first book on Austen, *Jane Austen and the
Body*, argues that Austen uses the "unhealthy body" as a
source of events in her fiction, and that bodies (especially in distress or ill health) are "sites in which cultural
meanings are inscribed." Extreme emotions—grief,
rage, despair, loneliness—which are socially repressed
or censored find their expression as physical symptoms.
Wiltshire is drawing on Arthur Kleinman's theory of
"somatisation," in which illness is thought of as a language for what is being repressed: "emotions are deposited in the body and there reproduced as illness
symptoms." For Austen's female characters illness may
be their only way of getting their emotions "legitimised
and respected"—as with Jane Fairfax in *Emma*, who
seems at one point to be having a severe physical breakdown or episode of "neurasthenia," and who can only
express her concealed distress in this fashion. Wiltshire
doesn't mention Jane Austen's faint, but it could be the
perfect example of a repressed or restricted emotional
life finding its only possible outlet in a dramatic act of
bodily weakness.[22]

The interpretation of the faint will depend on what
kind of Austen is being purveyed. Obviously, readers who
identify Austen with the "green core," with the rural, se-
cluded heartland of England, and who read her life and
character as quiet, static, regional, and domestic, will as-
sume that enforced removal to town life would come as
an unpleasant shock, and they point to evidence from the
novels (particularly *Persuasion*) for her dislike of Bath.
Critics who want to shift this family-derived version of
the "timid Austen trapped within a regard for the local
and familiar," resist the story of the faint. Deidre Lynch
pours scorn on those interwar commentators who maintained as "an article of faith" "Austen's home-loving at-
tachment to a green nook" and "who told and retold the
story of how Jane swooned when Reverend Austen an-
nounced his intention to move the family to Bath." Clara
Tuite, in her treatment of the "commodification" of
Austen, notes that Bath's use of Austen for its tourist industry has a been "a sore point for many Austen devotees,
particularly given the fact that Austen made some beautifully disparaging remarks about Bath, and was rumoured
in the family history to have fainted at the shock of the
news that she and her family were about to move there."
Margaret Kirkham, writing a revisionary feminist account of Austen in the 1980s, turns the whole story on its
head. It is important, she says, "because it illustrates the
way in which the life of the legendary Jane Austen has
been created." She notes that the 1913 *Life* tells us that
"tradition says that . . . Jane Austen fainted away" when
she heard the news. But when Austen's niece Caroline
Austen, daughter of James, wrote her 1869 letter describing the event, she inaccurately said that Cassandra was

present, and she didn't mention the faint. Her account reads: "My Mother [Mary Austen, née Lloyd] who was present said my Aunt was greatly distressed." It was the *Memoir*, followed by the Austen editor R. W. Chapman in 1948, that piled on the emotion: "We cannot doubt that the loss of her native country and of the multitude of associations which made up her girlish experience was exquisitely painful. Her feelings cannot have been less acute than Marianne's on leaving Norland, or Anne's on leaving Kellynch." But Kirkham, having unpicked the evidence, goes on to argue that Austen's silence after she got to Bath could have meant, not that she was depressed, but that she was busy enjoying herself.[23]

No biographer of Jane Austen leaves out the faint, but all of them have to decide what to do with the story. John Halperin, whose 1984 Jane Austen has been described as "consumed by smouldering resentment at her lot, incapable of love, and cynical about personal relationships," and whose biography was certainly setting out to disrupt previous readings of her life, makes the most of the drama, and writes as if with inside knowledge of her feelings, drawn from her novels:

> Jane fainted. She was not a fainter; the emotional disturbance must have been acute. Beneath her celebrated composure she was high-strung. And she was upset. It is significant that for December 1800 . . . there are no letters extant—bearing silent testimony, perhaps, to the novelist's agitated state of mind. . . . Did her feelings resemble those of Marianne Dashwood upon leaving Norland—or those of Anne Elliot upon leaving Kellynch? We shall never know. What we do know is that Steventon had been

everything to Jane Austen, and she never liked Bath; Anne Elliot . . . "persisted in a very determined, though silent, disinclination for Bath." All Jane's roots were at Steventon. . . . The novelist was "exceedingly unhappy" upon hearing the news, says the author of the *Memoir*, a man not given to exaggeration. There can be no doubt that she was unhappy. Indeed, she was to remain dissatisfied for a good many years. A decade of rootlessness was about to begin; this was a watershed event in her life.

Note the biographer's strategic uses of "must have" and "perhaps" and of rhetorical questions, the setting of unprovable hypotheses ("we shall never know") against resounding conclusions ("there can be no doubt." . . . "Indeed"), the ease with which evidence is adduced from the novels, and the tendency to trust the family version, as put together by R. W. Chapman and, later, Deirdre Le Faye—though Halperin goes on to dismiss the rumour that the Austen parents were trying to get her away from William Digweed. This passage comes in a chapter called "The Treacherous Years," in which Halperin argues that bitterness and dislocations clouded the "dark" years of 1801 to 1804, for which no letters remain, and that "adversity blanketed energy and inspiration." So he adopts the standard view that Jane Austen was acting out the feelings she gave to her heroines, and that to be uprooted from home was to be stopped in her creative flow. Readings of Austen's authorial career (such as Kathryn Sutherland's) which dispute the chronology of two bursts of creativity with a long fallow gap in between, arguing rather for a long period of literary experimentation, will not accept this version.

Park Honan's 1987 *Jane Austen*, which places her more thoroughly in her social and political context, uses the sources more carefully, but comes to similar conclusions:

> At this news Jane Austen fainted, so Anna Lefroy heard. ... Cassandra was absent when the decision was made, and Mary Austen found Jane quite alone and "greatly distressed"—but a younger daughter's tears were insignificant. Aunt Perrot knew or imagined why Jane was "distressed." The family *had* to move, that lady felt, because of a romantic attachment between Jane and a Digweed man. What could one expect? But dear Jane would forget her suitor when she was living at Axford Buildings in Bath. ... In leaving Steventon she was being uprooted and crushed. ... She was being taken from a small community, which she knew well. ... There could be no compensation in a jangling crowded town. Her sense of place was part of her confidence, and *that* was being torn from her. One could be sad in leaving a place because connections are cut *too* easily: other people part from one too readily, and friendships are exposed as less significant than one had hoped and perhaps as insignificant as they really are. But the precious intimacy of talk and feeling she had with Martha [Lloyd] or Catherine [Bigg] or Mrs Lefroy was rare, and it was cruel to leave. A loss may be a gain, but how does one happily endure without love, friendship, peace and delight? ... She meant to be cheerful but until well into January 1801 she found little to allay what Mary called her "distress."

The tactic here seems to be a pretence at writing an eighteenth-century novel, perhaps a novel by Jane Austen, in which some of the facts are given to us from the imagined viewpoint of Aunt Perrot, and the events provide an excuse for a general meditation on uprootings.[24]

Two British lives of Jane Austen came out in 1997, one by Claire Tomalin and one by David Nokes. Both give us a troubling and troubled Austen, placed in a discordant and dangerous late eighteenth-century English landscape, and belonging to a family with some dubious secrets and connections. Yet their treatment of her life—and of her faint—could hardly be more different, though they are using much the same materials and evidence.

Claire Tomalin's biography is interested in the story of a woman's life, and how to tell it. What effect would being fostered by a wet-nurse have on a baby girl? Might it create a lifelong defensiveness and an emotional distance between mother and child? What would be the toughening results of being sent away to school very young? What would it feel like to be a teenage girl starting to menstruate surrounded by young boys "thundering about the house"? Is it anachronistic to feel pity for young wives pregnant immediately after marriage, and then every year, and often dying in childbirth? (Austen did: "Poor Animal, she will be worn out before she is thirty," she wrote of her niece Anna Lefroy, pregnant again in 1816 immediately after the birth of her first child.) Women's feelings—about the pleasures of dancing or the imprisoning effects of bad weather—are constantly conjectured. Tomalin sees, as others have, conflict and exasperation with the strong, stubborn mother. She casts some shadow over the quasi-marital closeness with Cassandra, who is viewed as sombre, prim, and responsible for hurrying them both into middle age. (Tomalin finds the story of their wearing identical bonnets in their mid-twenties "depressing.") The key word in this biography (there always is one) is *tough*. This Austen is a witty, ebullient girl taking a series of knocks. The brief youthful flirtation with Tom Lefroy is dealt with tenderly, as is her painful change of mind over a later proposal. This is not, though, the standard male version of the embittered old maid who longed above all else to be married. Here Jane Austen is imagined as discovering that "spinsterhood . . . could be a form of freedom". The worst pressures are those of family life: lack of independence and privacy, endless domestic commitments, and feeling like an "awkward parcel" at the grander homes of her wealthier brothers.

Tomalin's version of the faint deals carefully with the possible motives of the Austen parents and with the sources: "This is Mary Austen's account, who was there; and although she misremembered the presence of Cassandra, there is no reason to doubt the truth of it. . . . James's daughter Anna was told her Aunt Jane fainted. Whether she did or not, it can hardly be doubted that the whole thing was a shock, and a painful one." There follows an account of the arrangements for the move, and a suggestion that the letters Cassandra destroyed immediately after the event may have been "too full of raw feeling and even anger."

> She strained to keep up the easy, gossipy note . . . but the jokes to Cass often feel forced: ". . . It must not be generally known however that I am not sacrificing a great deal in quitting the Country—or I can expect to inspire no tenderness, no interest in those we leave behind." . . . There

is a briskness and brightness in Jane's letters at this time, much keeping up of spirits, but no enthusiasm. She is doing what she has to do, making the best of a situation over which she has no control, watching the breaking up of everything familiar . . . fitting in with plans in which she has no say, losing what she loves for the prospect of an urban life . . . no centre, no peace, and the loss of an infinite number of things hard to list, impossible to explain.

Looking ahead over the silence that followed, Tomalin constructs a whole theory of depression:

> The ejection from Steventon made severe practical difficulties for her; it also depressed her deeply enough to disable her as a writer. Depression may be set off when a bad experience is repeated, and it seems likely that this is what happened here. First as an infant, then as a child of seven, Jane had been sent away from home, frightening and unpleasant experiences over which she had no control. . . . Through her writing, she was developing a world of imagination in which she controlled everything that happened. She went on to create young women somewhat like herself, but whose perceptions and judgements were shown to matter; who were able to influence their own fates significantly. . . . To remove her from Steventon would destroy the delicate balance she had worked out. . . . So there was both a perfectly good rational basis for wanting to be at home, and a residue of the terrors of infancy and childhood about banishment and exile, ready to spring out when they threatened again. That this new exile was brought about by the same people as before, her parents, against whom she could neither rebel nor complain, must have made it worse. . . . Her account of Fanny's permanent

low spirits after a childhood trauma, and her very different
account (in *Sense and Sensibility*) of Marianne unable to
combat her misery and willing herself into serious illness,
show how well she understood depression. And however
she dealt with and controlled her own, it struck at the core
of her being: it interfered directly with her power to write.[25]

It is a highly plausible version, made all the more so by
the sympathetic narrative of a woman's life that surrounds it, and by cunning little touches like the use of
"Cass" and "Jane" to suggest inwardness, the biographical hooks for plausibility ("seems likely," "must have"),
and the reasonable demonstration of links between the
work and the life. All the same, it is entirely constructed
and hypothetical, just as much of a figment as the "dear
Aunt Jane" of the family *Memoir*, but this one—like
many other twentieth-century biographies—is dependent on our accepting post-Freudian psychoanalytical
terms (loss of control, the repeating of "childhood
trauma," willing oneself into illness) for an eighteenth-
century writer.

Tomalin's version was influential on the novelist Carol
Shields, who pays close attention in her short biography
to the bodily features and body parts in Austen's work.
She argues that there are so few references to bodily acts
or images in the novels that "the rarity of such allusions
sometimes gives them power, as though minor physical
allusions are code words for larger sensations." All the
same, she is dubious about the faint: "Can she really
have fainted, she who in her earliest work mocked ex-
travagant emotional responses, especially those assigned
to women?" She draws attention to the unreliability of

the evidence ("not securely embedded in eye-witness reports . . . the story is muddled and riddled with inconsistencies"), and notes that unanswered questions remain: "Did other choices occur to her? Were other possibilities offered?" Still, her main line agrees with Tomalin's, that this was a painful uprooting which "would have required extraordinary feats of adjustment." She imagines Jane Austen "swallowing hard" and trying to make that adjustment; she thinks the letters to Cassandra sound "merry and expectant and feverishly false," and she agrees with Tomalin that "there can be little question that Jane Austen's rather fragile frame of creativity was disturbed following the move to Bath."[26]

Almost all biographies, when the subject undergoes pain or suffering, look for someone to blame, and David Nokes, whose combative life came out in the same year as Claire Tomalin's, puts the blame firmly on the Austens, whom he vilifies as a crew of snobbish, greedy, competitive entrepreneurs. Their "habit of suppressing awkward or embarrassing facts" (such as Jane's "mad" brother George, sent away from home as an infant and never afterwards referred to, or Jane's aunt, Mrs. Leigh-Perrot, standing trial for grand larceny), and their "idealization of Jane Austen's posthumous reputation" "has had its inevitable effect on subsequent biographies," says Nokes. He sets out to undercut this "policy of censorship" and to present a more alarming Austen. He sees her as deeply unromantic: malevolently resentful of the privations of her life, pleasure-loving and malicious. The mysterious Devonshire clergyman, according to Nokes, was probably an invention of Cassandra's. (Possibly, he argues, Cassandra and Jane didn't get on as well as is generally thought: there may have been "rivalry—even treachery" between them.) This Jane Austen is more interested in amusement and self-advancement than romance. Far from contentedly living a quiet rural life, she couldn't wait to get away from it, and longed for wealth, luxury, and amusement. She was Mary Crawford, rather than Fanny Price. But Nokes also wants us to see her as a complicated and challenging human being, torn between self-punishment and self-conceit, and dangerously subversive of the pieties and moralities of her time. When she began to be known as an author and visited London, Austen expressed anxiety at the thought of being shown off as an exhibit. "If I *am* a wild beast, I cannot help it," she wrote to Cassandra from London in 1813. Nokes, who loves this quotation and frequently cites it out of context, calls her "rebellious, satirical and wild."

As all literary biographers must, he has to find a way of understanding the work's relation to the life, and his is to argue that Austen used the fiction as a form of punishment. So she invents a self-mortifying heroine, Fanny Price, as a way of rebuking her own desire for fame, success, and entertainment. Or else the novels work as "vicarious gratification." For all Nokes's robust iconoclasm, his desire to rival Austen in empathy and imaginativeness leads him into some riskily fictional, even surprisingly sentimental and old-fashioned passages, as here, imagining Austen writing *Persuasion* at night and thinking back on the time when she gave in to family persuasion not to marry Tom Lefroy: "That night, as she lay on her bed, listening to the sound of the rain on the window pane, and feeling still the dull ache in her back, Jane allowed herself to imagine how it might have been. It was, at least, a kind of vicarious gratification to confer on her heroine the consummation that had always been denied to her."

If Nokes allows himself, here and there, a few moments of "Janeite" tenderness, he makes up for it by being very fierce and sardonic about the faint, which he uses as a weapon to beat all previous Austen biographers round the head with. "Jane Austen's fainting fit appears as a crucial traumatic event in all the traditional accounts of her life. Yet the authority for this story is not strong, and we might pause to query why it has found such widespread acceptance." He goes on to doubt the reliability of Caroline Austen's account, written at second hand so long after the event, and its embellishment, many years later, in the *Memoir*, where the faint is introduced. And he notes how eager "subsequent biographers" have been to accept this account:

> Austen's biographers have been happy to repeat a story which accords so well with their own views of how she *ought* to have felt. Imagine her anguish! To be torn away from the native Hampshire village that she loved and dragged away, against her will, to Bath, that fashionably soulless resort of quacks, hacks, thieves, conspirators and hypochondriacs. There is a tendency for them to wax indignant on her behalf at such a forced removal.

He quotes Deirdre Le Faye, Park Honan, and R. W. Chapman on her distress. "All these biographers," he adds, "note a significant gap in the sequence of letters between Jane and Cassandra at this time, and draw similar conclusions from it." But he has a different interpretation of the gap (very like Margaret Kirkham's, though he doesn't cite her): "Quite possibly the inadmissible sentiments which Cassandra chose to suppress were those of an unseemly excitement." He quotes the letter to Cassandra of January 1801 which Le Faye and Tomalin and others quote: "It must not be generally known that I am not sacrificing a great deal in quitting the country—or I can expect to inspire no tenderness, no interest in those we leave behind." But Nokes reads it differently:

> This is not the language of someone who feels crushed, grief-stricken or incarcerated. ... For years Jane had dreamt of a larger world, where she might savour the luxury of well-proportioned rooms, or indulge a taste for wild coach-rides. On her visit to Bath two summers earlier, she had thrown herself with some energy into the excitement of gala concerts, fireworks, shopping and scandal.

Perhaps the silence of the Bath and Southampton years, which biographers have used "to confirm their sense of the feelings of unhappiness and displacement which she must have experienced in these busy cities," was actually due to the fact that this Jane Austen, a good-time girl, was having such a busy and social urban life that she had no time for writing: "Happiness may be just as destructive of literary dedication as unhappiness. And it is equally possible to suggest that it was an abundance of amusements, rather than the absence of inspiration, that prevented her from writing."[27]

This is more exciting, but just as hypothetical, as the versions which construct depression from the gaps and silences. It provides an intriguing example of quite contrary interpretations of a life from much the same data.

Read alongside each other, and set in the context of the long and continuing battles for possession of the posthumous body of Jane Austen, these two biographies provide a riveting example of biography as a relativist process of conjecture, invention, intuition, and manipulation of the evidence. They also point to the mystery of lives, which Austen, for all her penetrating analytical abilities and comic control, often invokes. John Wiltshire notes drily: "We actually know much less about Jane Austen than her biographers would have us believe."[28] And that resistance to being known is something the novelist herself was interested in. Mrs. Smith can produce the evidence (even from dubious lower-class sources) of Mr. Elliot's villainy, and can confirm Anne's doubts about him: proof, witness, demonstration, seem incontrovertible. But what isn't so clearly explained is, for instance, why she takes so long to give Anne this information, or what her motives are, or what kind of pleasure Anne gets out of visiting her. One of the things Austen's novels do is to make us understand how difficult it is to know other people right through. As Fanny Price exclaims to Mary Crawford in the shrubbery in *Mansfield Park*[29] (though she isn't really listening), how incomprehensible the human mind is, and how "peculiarly past finding out"!

Chapter 4

....

How to End It All

Most (though not all) biographies are about the dead. Most biographers, therefore, have to decide how to deal with the death of their subject. But why "deal with"? Doesn't biography just state the facts? No, because there is a great deal invested, always, in the death of the subject, in terms of how the death relates to the life, how the subject behaves at their death, and how, if at all, the death can be interpreted. There are also tricky questions for the biographer about tone of voice at the moment of the subject's death. If you are coming to the end of a life you've spent a lot of time with, you will tend to be moved—if only by relief. Do you let these emotions flood the page, hoping they will flood the reader, too? Do you restrain your emotions and give the death clinically? If you are writing the life of a writer, do you allow yourself to describe their death as they might have done it in their fictions or poetry? Do you, in the tone you choose, and also in matters of structure and interpretation, try to give the death meaning and derive from it some sense of a resolution of the life?

The answers to these questions will depend very much on when, and in what cultural context, the Life is being

written. One model for changing attitudes to death, suggestive and influential, if not entirely convincing, was
provided by the French social historian Philippe Ariès's
books *Western Attitudes towards Death* (1976) and *The
Hour of Our Death* (1981), with sources drawn mainly
from French Catholic culture. Ariès famously proposed
four broad historical phases of attitudes towards death.

In the first, in the early Medieval period—his evidence
comes from French Romances of the tenth, eleventh,
and twelfth centuries—there was what he calls "tame or
tamed death." "Death was a ritual organised by the dying
person himself." It was witnessed by family, friends, and
neighbours, and was dealt with as a communal ceremony
expressing "resignation to the collective destiny of
the species." In the second, in the later Medieval period,
the dying person is still presiding over the event, but the
rise of individualism undermines the calm acceptance of
death. Ariès calls this "the death of the self" ("la mort de
soi"), in which there is an increasingly close relationship
between "death and the biography of each individual
life." This way of thinking about death, Ariès argues,
dominated until the eighteenth century, when a third
phase takes over, characterised by an idea of "la mort de
toi," the death of the other, or "the beautiful death."
A romantic, emotional, even erotic, rhetoric of loss and
bereavement makes itself felt on tombstones and in epi-
taphs. More crying and fainting went on at deathbeds,
and "the cult of memory" developed.[1] In the fourth
phase, which Ariès identifies as postindustrial and contemporaneous, death is made "invisible," taboo, hushed
up, "unnameable," hidden away in hospitals. The dying
are no longer told that they are dying, and so cannot

prepare their farewells. "She didn't even say goodbye to us," Ariès quotes a son saying at the bedside of his mother." Excessive mourning is felt to be morbid, children are protected from deathbed scenes, and it becomes indecent to let someone die in public.[2]

Many historians of social rituals of death have quarrelled with Ariès's broad-brush historical divisions.[3] Pat Jalland notes that the Evangelical model of the "good death" is more apt for Protestant nineteenth-century England than Ariès's "beautiful death," and was in any case in decline by the end of the century. John Wolffe argues that there was, in fact, "no normative or ideal model" for deathbed behaviour in Britain in the nineteenth century. Douglas Davies, in *Death, Ritual and Belief*, is suspicious of Ariès's sweeping generalisation. But he does agree that the idea of how much "control" we can have over our own deathbeds has always been a crucial part of social and cultural attitudes to dying.[4]

We would now want to add a contemporaneous phase to Ariès's periods of death, a phase in which the deaths of ordinary people are made public. This phase or moment has been made all too memorable for us by the events of 11 September 2001, since we have all shared the last words, most often words of love, which the victims of the attack spoke on their phones from the Twin Towers and from the hijacked planes. And we have become "used," if used is the word to use, to hearing the last words of pilots in air crashes relayed from black box readings; many can remember reading the letter left for his loved one by a young Russian seaman perishing in the Kursk submarine. British readers in the 1990s shared the banal, everyday "dying" experiences of journalists such as Ruth Picardie or John Diamond, whose publicly recorded stages of dying from cancer may have provided consolation to others in similar situations.

The search for exemplary deaths has a very long history. Now we find it in ordinary people's lives, not in saints' or great men's lives. But our continuing interest in exemplary deaths, "good deaths," goes back to medieval stories of "holy living and holy dying," and to the handbooks for exemplary deaths, the *ars moriendi* of the fifteenth century. The *Arte and Crafte to Know Well to Dye* of 1490 included instruction such as: "To die well is to die gladly." The exemplary death of a great man continues to impress, even when the death is not "holy." In the eighteenth century, both Boswell and the economist Adam Smith gave accounts of the death of the philosopher David Hume. The firm-minded Hume, renowned for his atheism, refused all false consolation on his deathbed in 1776 ("Your hopes are groundless," he said to Adam Smith). Questioned anxiously by Boswell about immortality at their last meeting, Hume good-humouredly maintained his sceptical position: "I asked him if the thought of Annihilation never gave him any uneasiness. He said not the least; no more than the thought that he had not been, as Lucretius observes." Hume's death as a sceptic is rendered, both by Smith and Boswell, as a heroic, even saintly death. (Boswell and Johnson argued over it: Johnson's opinion was that Hume was lying if he said he didn't fear death.)[5]

In nineteenth-century Evangelical England, the secular Lives of great men—statesmen, leaders, educationalists, politicians—were often coloured by features inherited from saints' lives or classical models. In such narratives death must be heroic, must provide a lesson; a "good death" is of the utmost importance, and "last words" needed to be witnessed and reported. John Wolffe, in his book on the subject, *Great Deaths*, describes the widespread interest in the last moments of royalty and public figures. Disraeli's death in 1881 was a focus of "sustained public interest": people wanted to know if it was "a close worthy of the wonderful life." Gladstone's death in 1898, a slow and horribly painful death from cancer of the mouth, was sanitised in public accounts to show "how a Christian should die." John Morley wrote an idealised deathbed scene in his *Life of Gladstone* of 1904, responding to Gladstone's daughter's plea that his suffering should not be publicly aired.[6] And there are many more examples of saintly nineteenth-century deaths. One is in Dean Stanley's 1844 *Life* of his legendary teacher Thomas Arnold, headmaster of Rugby. The book ends with a tremendously pious and prolonged deathbed scene, in which Dr. Arnold, dying of a heart attack at the age of forty-seven with his family around him, thanks God for giving him this pain which is so good for him. Another is in Robert Southey's *Life of Nelson* (1832), a book which was intended as "a manual for the young sailor, which he may carry about with him, till he has treasured up the example in his memory and his heart." (It was published in a handy pocket-size edition for that purpose—no doubt to be whipped out on board ship in the middle of a battle or a thunderstorm to see what Nelson would have done in such circumstances.) Nelson's death in battle is a saint's death which gives the conclusive meaning to his life. His dying words on deck, barely discernible to the listeners, were, not "Kiss me Hardy," but, "Thank God I have done my duty . . . God and my country." Nelson, the author concludes, provides "a name and an example, which are at this hour inspiring thousands of the youth of England, a name which is our pride, and an example which will continue to be our sword and shield."[7]

Out of that tradition of exemplary deaths comes the curious vogue for anthologies of death, which persisted into the twentieth century. Victorian Evangelical tracts published consoling last words, some more elevated than others; Pat Jalland quotes an 1880s memoir of the Evangelical Caroline Leakey, *Clear Shining Light*, whose last words were: "Farewell, dear drawing-room, you have long been devoted to God."[8] Anthologies of the literature of death, like *The Art of Dying* (1930), or D. J. Enright's *Oxford Book of Death* (1983) include,[9] or are made up of, selections of famous last words. D. J. Enright is particularly keen on the "last words" which sum up a person's work or seem to "predicate a continuity of occupation between this life and the next," like Gainsborough's "We are all going to heaven, and Van Dyck is of the company" (1788), Beethoven's "I shall hear in Heaven" (1827), Adam Smith's "I believe we must adjourn this meeting to some other place" (1790), or Turner's "The Sun is God" (1851). Enright observes that we have become more cynical about legendary, overapposite last words, which may well have been invented or embellished by a ghostwriter, though, as he says, it is still nice to think that Andrew Bradford, an eighteenth-century Philadelphian newspaper publisher, did cry on his deathbed, "Oh Lord, forgive the errata!"

And, echoing Ariès, he notes that the hospitalisation and, very often, the sedation of the dying have led to the "dying out" of last words as an institution.[10]

Janet Malcolm, much of whose work attacks biographical inventions and intrusions, gives a sardonic warning in *Reading Chekhov* (2003) of how our fascination with last words can lead to myth-making and inaccuracy. Chekhov's death, she writes, "is one of the great set-pieces of literary history." It is recorded in an account written by his wife, Olga Knipper, four years after the death, which took place on 2 July 1904. The Chekhovs were in a German hotel. The dying Chekhov woke up in the night and asked for a doctor. Olga asked a Russian student, Rabeneck, who was in the hotel, to go for the doctor. The doctor came, and cradled Chekhov in his arms. Chekhov said "Ich sterbe" (I am dying). The doctor gave him an injection of camphor, and ordered champagne. Olga writes:

> Anton took a full glass, examined it, smiled at me, and said: "It's a long time since I drank champagne." He drained it, lay quietly on his left side, and I just had time to run to him and lean across the bed, and call to him, but he had stopped breathing and was sleeping peacefully as a child.

Later, in 1922, Olga embellished the account, adding a moth flying into the room after the death, the cork bursting out of the champagne bottle, an expression of serenity on the dead man's face, and the waking song of the birds. The student Rabeneck also wrote an account, fifty-four years after the death, which adds more details: the doctor sending him for oxygen, a "strange sound coming from Chekhov's throat," and the doctor asking

Rabeneck to tell Olga that Chekhov is dead. The doctor also left a (second-hand) report, which had Chekhov saying "Soon, doctor, I am going to die," and his reaction to the doctor saying he will send for oxygen: "Before they brought the oxygen, I would be dead." Another second-hand account, from a Russian journalist called Iollos, who interviewed Olga on the day of Chekhov's death, added still more details. Chekhov was raving, saying something about a sailor, something about the Japanese. Then, Olga was putting an ice pack on Chekhov's chest, and he said with a sad smile: "You don't put ice on an empty heart." Iollos says that Chekhov's last words were "Ich sterbe": nothing about the champagne.

Malcolm goes on to look at how biographers of Chekhov have treated their sources, and finds all kinds of inventions and elaborations, for instance in David Magarshack's *Anton Chekhov: A Life* (1952):

> Chekhov said with a smile, "It's a long time since I drank champagne." He had a few sips and fell back on the pillow. Soon he began to ramble. "Has the sailor gone? Which sailor?" He was apparently thinking of the Russo-Japanese war. . . . This went on for several minutes. His last words were "I'm dying"; then in a very low voice to the doctor in German: "Ich sterbe." . . . Suddenly, without uttering a sound, he fell sideways. He was dead. His face looked very young.

Other examples, listed by Malcolm—from lives of Chekhov by Princess Toumanova (1937), Daniel Gilles (1967), Henri Troyat (1984), Irene Nemirovsky (1950), V. S. Pritchett (1988), Donald Rayfield (1997), and Philip Callow (1998)—add all kinds of extras. "Don't put ice on an empty heart" gets turned into "Don't put ice on an empty stomach." Chekhov's eyes glitter, the moth flies round the room while he is dying, the sailor becomes his nephew, or a character in the story "Ward 6." Philip Callow, in particular, splashes on the details, for instance about the champagne: "The doctor . . . went to the telephone in the alcove and ordered a bottle of the hotel's best champagne. He was asked how many glasses. 'Three,' he shouted, 'and hurry, d'you hear?'" And the champagne arrives with cut-crystal glasses carried by "a sleepy young porter." Reading this, Malcolm suddenly remembered a story she had read by Raymond Carver, called "Errand," in the 1989 collection *Where I'm Calling From*, which makes up the details of Chekhov's death, just as Philip Callow gives them. She is bewildered—and offended—by all these fictionalisations. But what her fascinating comparative account makes clear is that all biographers want to make as much as possible of the ending of the life. It matters to us, as Chekhov's readers, whether his last words really were (as we would like them to be), "It's a long time since I drank champagne."[11]

We still have a great preoccupation with endings, and when I read European or Anglo-American biographies, of the past and of the present, it seems to me that, for all Ariès's neat division into four "phases" of thinking about death, there is, particularly in post-nineteenth-century biography, a confused and complicated mixture of ideas about how dying relates to a life-story. But why should the manner of the death and the explanations for the death of the subject still matter so much? Why should there still be so much pressure on the biographer to read the whole life of the subject in terms of the death (especially if that death is a suicide)? The Christian tradition, which has had a profound bearing on the history of Western biography, and which explains our lasting curiosity about last words, still makes us want the death to complete the meaning of the life. The desire reflects, in Frank Kermode's phrase in *The Sense of an Ending*, "our deep need for intelligible Ends."[12] We prefer not to read the subject's death, as perhaps it should be read, as without content, merely contingent, just the next fact in a series of facts: to "de-dramatize it," as Edmund White quotes Genet as saying.[13] We feel we must stage it and interpret it, or overinterpret it. In Julian Barnes's novel *Flaubert's Parrot*, an obscure critic called Edmund Ledoux is mocked for devising an influential legend that Flaubert committed suicide, thereby ignoring the literary evidence "of a man whose stoicism runs as deep as his pessimism":

> Ledoux's account of the suicide goes like this: Flaubert *hanged himself in his bath*. I suppose it's more plausible than saying that he electrocuted himself with sleeping pills; but really. . . . What happened was this. Flaubert got up, took a hot bath, had an apoplectic fit, and stumbled to a sofa in his study; there he was found expiring by the doctor who later issued the death certificate. That's what happened. End of story. Flaubert's earliest biographer talked to the doctor concerned and that's that. Ledoux's version requires the following chain of events: Flaubert got into his hot bath, hanged himself in some as yet unexplained fashion, then climbed out, hid the rope, staggered to his study, collapsed on the sofa and, when the doctor arrived, managed

to die while feigning the symptoms of an apoplectic fit. Really, it's too ridiculous.[14]

"That's what happened"; "End of story"; "that's that"—death as just a fact is wittily set against the "ridiculous" overinterpretation of M. Ledoux. But we have still not reached a point, in the writing and reading of life-stories, where "end of story" is a neutral or simple moment. There are conflicting ways of thinking about death, mixed together in biographers' choices about how to end it all.

In Lytton Strachey's early twentieth-century biographical writing, which set out to debunk the kind of exemplary hagiography that we find in Stanley's *Life of Arnold* (Strachey's own sketch of Arnold in *Eminent Victorians* [1918] marks the difference), things are not as clear-cut, when it comes to dying, as Strachey might have wanted them to be. Here is his 1921 account of the death of Queen Victoria:

> She herself, as she lay blind and silent, seemed to those who watched her to be divested of all thinking—to have glided already, unawares, into oblivion. Yet, perhaps, in the secret chambers of consciousness, she had her thoughts, too. Perhaps her fading mind called up once more the shadows of the past to float before it, and retraced, for the last time, the vanished visions of that long history—passing back and back, through the cloud of years to older and ever older memories—to the spring woods at Osborne, so full of primroses for Lord Beaconsfield—to Lord Palmerston's queer clothes and high demeanour, and Albert's face under the green lamp, and Albert's first stag at Balmoral, and Albert in his blue and silver uniform . . .

and Lord M dreaming at Windsor with the rooks cawing
in the elm-trees . . . and her mother's features sweeping
down towards her, and a great old repeater-watch of her
father's in its tortoise-shell case, and a yellow rug, and
some friendly flounces of sprigged muslin, and the trees
and the grass at Kensington.[15]

And that's how his book ends. Strachey is trying out a
new psychoanalytical model on the venerable Queen of
England which must, at the time (only twenty years after
her death) have been rather startling. She becomes just
another human being, as her whole life flashes before
her eyes, and her involuntary memories rush her back to
the primal scene of childhood. But if this is a debunking
mechanism, it is also a surprisingly sentimental piece of
writing, allowing in, at the very last, the Victorian ele-
giac pathos Strachey has been so keen to satirise in his
treatment of the age. Bruce Redford, writing on
Boswell's *Life of Johnson* and on the fictive methods of biography, in *Designing the Life of Johnson* (2002), calls this
"a vivid montage," an invitation "to relive his biography
at top speed." But, he says, "the flashback sacrifices history to poetry . . . [and] distances us by making the versa-
tile biographer the true protagonist of his tale." It "sacrifices credibility to pyrotechnic display."[16]

In contemporary biographies, especially of literary figures, you may still find that attempt to stage the whole
meaning of the life and the life's work at the deathbed,
sometimes with unfortunate effects, as in the ending of
John Halperin's 1984 *Life* of Jane Austen:

From 7 p.m. on 17 July until she died the next morning
at 4:30 a.m. in the arms of her sister, Jane Austen, after

praying for death, lay apparently insensible. What thoughts, if any, may have raced through the fading light of her mind we of course shall never know. Did she, perhaps, dream of Chawton, its paths and gardens, and wonder how her mother might greet the news of her death? Did she recall that wonderful moonlit walk she took from Alton to Chawton the previous autumn, when, for the last time, she seemed to possess all her strength? Did her thoughts stray back to that tumultuous trip to London in the autumn of 1815 ... ? ... Did she remember the arrival of her "favourite child" *Pride and Prejudice* from London in 1813, or the excitement of holding her very first publication in her hands in 1811, or the years of "exile" in Southampton and Bath which preceded that first success? ... Did she recall the awful night at Manydown when she changed her mind about marriage ... ? Did she dream of that vibrant autumn of 1800, when she danced her feet off at the Basingstoke ball ... ? ... Did her thoughts wander back to Steventon, its shrubbery and its country walks ... bittersweet memories of a boy named Tom who had first touched her heart? ... How would her brothers and their children respond to the news of her death; how would her sister take it? Surely some portion of her last earthly thoughts must have been of Cassandra, with whom she had always shared everything; Cassandra, who seemed always to be there, as she was now; Cassandra, in whose arms she lay cradled; Cassandra; Cassandra.[17]

Like Strachey, Halperin runs backwards through the life as it flashes past, but it reads as a clumsy, laboriously rhetorical device for reminding his readers of the main events, and an intolerably sentimental fictionalising of his heroine. D. J. Taylor does the same thing, rather

oddly, at the end of his otherwise matter-of-fact *Life* of
George Orwell (2003). The italicised passage here seems
to add nothing more to our sense of Orwell's life than a
redundant, if stylish, tribute to Strachey:[18]

"Orwell's Dream"

> *And perhaps at the very end his mind moved back, back
> through the cloud of the years, to older and even older memories:
> to the rain falling over the grey sea off Jura; to the thump of the
> bombs going off in the streets beyond Piccadilly; and the lofted
> torches in the great square at Barcelona; and the electric shock of
> the bullet slamming home; and Eileen's face under the church
> gate; and Eileen at the supper table in Hampstead . . . and his
> mother's shadow falling across the garden; and the sound of the
> nightjars on summer evenings in the lanes; and the woods and
> the streams of Oxfordshire.*

All of these biographers are using the same strategy to
make the moment of their subject's death sum up and
conclude the whole story of their life. Where biography
leans towards fiction, this is a favoured tactic. The novelist Peter Ackroyd, in his *Life* of Dickens (1990), brings in
all the characters of Dickens's imagination to witness his
death, and uses a similar device of accumulative rhetorical questions to make the fantasy work. In Ackroyd's the-
atrical staging, Dickens is, at his death, at the centre of
the world he himself has created. Ackroyd makes much
of the last words.

> "On the ground." His last words. And is it possible that he
> had in some bewildered way echoed the words of Louisa
> Gradgrind to her errant father in *Hard Times*, "I shall die
> if you hold me! Let me fall upon the ground!"? And were

his other characters around him as he lay unconscious
through his last night? . . . And can we see them now, the
ghosts of Dickens's imagination, hovering around him as
he approaches his own death? Oliver Twist, Ebenezer
Scrooge, Paul Dombey, Little Nell, Little Dorrit, The
Artful Dodger, Bob Sawyer, Sam Weller, Mr Pickwick
[thirty-two more names of Dickens's characters follow] . . .
all of them now hovering around their creator as his life
on earth came to an end.[19]

As well as giving to the death the conclusive meaning of
the life's work, Ackroyd is also trying to emulate and
even parody his subject's literary strategies and his language. (That overlap of tone between biographer and
subject is often noticeable in nineteenth-century life-
writing, less so, usually, in later biography.)[20] And he is
also bringing his biography full circle, since he began his
book with the writer on his deathbed, having his death-
mask taken, so as to establish the myth of a Dickens who
always connected death and infancy and who feared
more than anything the return of the dead.[21] Both
Halperin and Ackroyd fictionalize their deathbed scenes,
in attempts to be "true," not to the realities of death, but
to the spirit of the writer's life. The opposite of this is the
biography that tries to unpick false or legendary associations of the life with the work or the myths which have
accumulated around the writer's death, like Richard
Holmes's account of the death of Shelley (with which I
began this book), or Claire Tomalin's revisionary account
of Dickens's death in *The Invisible Woman*, or Juliet
Barker's realistic, demystifying account of Emily Brontë's
death in *The Brontës* (1994). This is a dry, exact, scrupulously evidence-based account, which still can't quite

resist invoking the spirit of Emily Brontë's own work. It is worth quoting at length, since it works through the slow, dogged accumulation of detail:[22]

Emily was now in the final stages of consumption, though neither she nor her family apparently suspected how close she was to death. Though the pain in her side and chest had improved, her cough, shortness of breath and extreme emaciation had not; to add to her troubles, she began to suffer from diarrhoea, though she remained adamant that "no poisoning doctor" should come near her. "Never in all her life had she lingered over any task that lay before her, and she did not linger now," Charlotte later wrote of her sister. . . . The evening before her death, she insisted on feeding the dogs, Keeper and Flossy, as she had always done. As she stepped from the warmth of the kitchen into the cold air of the damp, stone-flagged passage, she staggered and almost fell against the wall. Charlotte and Anne, rushing to help her, were brushed aside and, recovering herself, she went on to give the dogs their dinner. Mrs Gaskell reported how Charlotte shivered recalling the pang she had felt when, having searched over the bleak December moors for a single sprig of heather to take in to Emily, she realised that her sister had not even recognised her favourite flower. On the morning of Tuesday, 19 December 1848, she insisted on rising at seven as was her habit. Combing her hair before the fire, the comb slipped from her fingers and fell into the hearth; she was too weak to pick it up, and before Martha Brown arrived and retrieved it for her, a large part of it had been burnt away by the flames. Neither Martha nor Charlotte dared to offer assistance as Emily slowly dressed herself and made her way downstairs. Still struggling to keep up an appearance of normality, she even attempted to pick up her sewing . . .

By midday, Emily was worse. Her unbending spirit finally broken, she whispered between gasps for breath, "If you will send for a doctor, I will see him now." Dr Wheelhouse was summoned immediately but, of course, it was too late: there was nothing he could do. Tradition has it that Emily refused to the last to retire to bed, dying, as unconventionally as she had lived, on the sofa in the parsonage dining room. This seems unlikely, as there is no contemporary source for the story and Charlotte later movingly described how Emily's dog Keeper "lay at the side of her dying-bed." In all probability, therefore, Emily was carried upstairs to her own little room over the hall, which had once been the "children's study." . . . She fought death to the end. And it was a bitter end. There was no time for consolatory words or acceptance of the inevitable. After "a hard, short conflict," Emily was torn from the world, "turning her dying eyes reluctantly from the pleasant sun." At two o'clock in the afternoon, aged thirty, she died: the relentless conflict between strangely strong spirit and fragile frame was over.

Note "This seems unlikely." Barker (whose vast book on the Brontë sisters sets out to correct all previous versions of their lives, especially idealised accounts of Charlotte) will not be moved by the popular myth. She is like Janet Malcolm, refusing to accept unquestioningly the legendary story about Chekhov and the champagne. Barker takes care to provide her source-materials—all the more poignant because so scrupulously placed, as with Gaskell's reminiscence of Charlotte's evidence about Emily not recognising her favourite flower. Yet Barker is not entirely clinical, after all, in her retelling of this agonising story. There's a definite symbolic touching-up of that comb, "burnt away by the flames." And she allows echoes from Emily's own poetry to infiltrate, at the last, this apparently clinical narrative. The struggle in Brontë's poem "The Philosopher" between the "quenchless will" and the "little frame," and the dauntlessness of "no coward soul is mine," are deliberately echoed.

A desire to echo the subject's tone, in a spirit of tenderness and sympathy, is often heard in the closing pages of *Lives* of nineteenth-century writers. Victoria Glendinning's *Life* of Trollope (1992) ends like a Victorian novel, telling us what happens to all the characters, and concluding with the modest, affecting, and affectionate last words of Trollope's *Autobiography*: "Now I stretch out my hand, and from the further shore I bid adieu to all who have cared to read any among the many words that I have written."[23] Jenny Uglow's biography of Elizabeth Gaskell (1993) ends with a mention of one of the minor characters who appeared at her funeral at Knutsford: "And of all people, among the mourners was one of her protégés, Hamilton Aidé, who had walked across from Tatton. He was the man who wrote so badly but sang so beautifully, to Elizabeth's huge amusement. She would have liked that."[24] Her ending maintains to its very last word this biography's loving attention to detail, its tone of sympathy, attention, and humour—qualities which mirror Elizabeth Gaskell's own characteristics.

Such attempts, however scrupulous or persuasive, to make the moment of death somehow match up to, fulfil, or re-enact the imaginative life of the writer-subject can lead biographers of writers into difficulties. Proust is a particularly interesting case here, since so much of his writing is *about* death and our attitudes to it. Accounts of Proust's drawn out and heroic death (on 18 November 1922, from pneumonia, septicaemia, and damage to the lungs from asthma) by André Maurois (1950) and George Painter (1965) turn Proust into the writer as saint, meeting his end with "stoic disregard," "indescribable dignity," and "heroic courage."[25] Maurois cannot resist citing Proust's fictional account of the death of the writer Bergotte, in which the immortality of the artist is movingly suggested by the continuing existence of his books. Painter, whose whole thesis of the life of Proust is based on Proust's guilty love-hate relation with his mother, and on Proust's idea of "two paths" or "two ways," the natural self and the acquired self, interprets the death according to his thesis. Proust, he says, is supposed to have said "Mother" at the end. Painter comments: "Now only the young mother, restored from before the beginning of Time Lost, before she had ever seemed to withhold her love, remained. At half-past five, calm and motionless, his eyes still wide open, Proust died." Painter concludes: "As he predicted, the Two Ways had met . . . the self we are born with and the self which we acquire, always join at last."[26]

A dry warning note is sounded against that heroic, meaningful, anticipated, and resolved account of a writer's death, in which the life and the death are validated in terms of the work, in Beckett's 1965 essay on Proust, which he prefaces: "There is no allusion in this book to the legendary life and death of Marcel Proust,"

and in which he says this about death: "Whatever opinion we may be pleased to hold on the subject of death,
we may be sure that it is meaningless and valueless.
Death has not required us to keep a day free."[27] Jean-
Yves Tadié's 1996 biography of Proust seems to take
warning from Beckett in its attempt very scrupulously
and carefully to sort out the death from the writing. It
doesn't give "Mother" as a last word, and it doesn't try to
fit Proust's account of the death of Bergotte into his own
death.[28] Tadié is much more concerned with the story of
the writing life. He does note that Proust is writing sentences to do with the death of Bergotte on his own
deathbed. This includes a passage on the "frivolity of the
dying," where Bergotte, at his last gasp, is allowed to ask
for all the food and drink which had previously been
forbidden to him as a dead man. "I couldn't have some
champagne?" he asks. Perhaps he had been reading
about Chekhov.

Proust was violently opposed to biography, as many
novelists are, because it is a rival to their own art form.
These versions of Proust's death suggest, indeed, that it
is almost impossible for biographers not to try to be like
novelists, not to make the death of a writer simply a fact,
devoid of conclusive meanings or of relation to the
writer. Even when a modern, secular biographer is trying
to be completely clinical about their subject's death, to
describe it just in all its contingency and physical awful-
ness, it may still be hard to resist colouring the moment
of death with the subject's own attitude to death. The
poet and biographer Andrew Motion, in *Philip Larkin*
(1993), replaces sentiment with a mercilessly detailed account of every physical indignity of the death, but is still

writing—as is perhaps inevitable—in the shadow of the writer's own voice and feelings:

[In 1985] when Larkin should have been travelling to and from Buckingham Palace (to collect the Companion of Honour), he was at home, dazzled by fear and pain. The prospect of death, acknowledged but unnamed, raged out at him, concentrating the terrors he had kept before him all his life. ... In his fifties, the dread of oblivion darkened everything. Death, he said, "remains a sort of Bluebeard's Chamber in the mind, something one is *always* afraid of." As he entered his sixties his fear grew rapidly. Reviewing D. J. Enright's *Oxford Book of Death* in 1983 he said, "Man's most remarkable talent is for ignoring death. For once the certainty of permanent extinction is realized, only a more immediate calamity can dislodge it from the mind." ... Now he told Monica he was "spiralling down towards extinction." ... As Friday [28 November 1985] wore on Larkin grew steadily weaker. In the evening, trying to get into his chair in the sitting-room, he fell to the ground and picked himself up with difficulty. ... Later Larkin collapsed again in the downstairs lavatory, jamming the door shut with his feet. Monica was unable to force the door open. She couldn't even make him hear her—he had left his hearing-aid behind—but she could hear him. "Hot! Hot!" he was whispering pitifully. He had fallen with his face pressed to one of the central heating pipes that ran round the lavatory wall. The next door neighbour was called again, the door was opened, and Larkin was carried into the kitchen. He asked for some Complan. ... When the ambulance arrived he looked up at [Monica] wildly, begging her to destroy his diaries. [He is taken to hospital where he is heavily

sedated.] . . . Larkin had died at 1:24 a.m., turning to the
nurse who was with him, squeezing her hand, and saying
faintly, "I am going to the inevitable."[29]

Perhaps I should have called this essay "From Champagne to Complan." Yet even here, with all the clinical
detail and the physical humiliation—a far cry from
Arnold's or Nelson's heroic deaths, or Chekhov's romanticised last moments—there is still a belief in the significance and value of the last words, and an irresistible echo
of the work of the poet himself, in the phrases: "Dread of
oblivion darkened everything"; "Dazzled by fear and
pain"; and "Raged out at him." Larkin's biographer is
thinking of "Aubade":

> The dread
> Of dying, and being dead
> Flashes afresh to hold and horrify.
> Most things may never happen; this one will
> And realisation of it rages out
> In furnace fear when we are caught without
> People or drink.

And other lines from Larkin haunt this death-scene: "Why
aren't they screaming?" ("The Old Fools"); "Beneath it all,
desire of oblivion runs" ("Wants").

It is still unusual for contemporary biographers to ac-
cede to Beckett's idea of the meaninglessness and contingency of the death. Some twentieth-century biographies
of the most problematic figures of that century, such as
Stalin and Freud, still insist on the death as the moment
when the myth is fixed, or perpetuated—as though returning to Ariès's earliest "phase" in which the dying man

controls the event. Alan Bullock, in *Hitler and Stalin*, describes Stalin making a terrifying deathbed gesture, as
though "bringing down a curse" and thereby preserving
"his image of himself intact to the end." Peter Gay,
in *Freud: A Life for Our Time*, describes Freud's dying
gesture of "greetings, farewell, resignation," whereby
"the old stoic kept control of his life to the end."[30]

There is an interesting commentary on this dying gesture by Adam Phillips in "The Death of Freud," collected in *Darwin's Worms* (1999). Phillips argues that
Freud was preoccupied, bizarrely, with controlling his
own version of his life—bizarrely, since his life's work
was to ask "how do people become who they are" and
"what constitutes evidence for this." Yet he himself was
anxious to "keep control of the stories" that people
would tell about him. He destroyed his papers, and (like
Proust) he was extremely hostile to the idea of any biography. Biography, with its attempt to tell the conclusive
truth about a life—particularly the life of an artist—
seemed to Freud like a travesty or parody of psychoanalysis. Biography maintains, unlike psychoanalysis, that
the meaning of a life can be finalised. Biography dimin-
ishes or travesties the human project, which is "to die in
our own way." Freud wanted his death "to *belong* to
him," not to his biographers. What, then, asks Phillips,
do Freud's biographers, Ernest Jones and Peter Gay, do
with the death of Freud, a slow, torturing, lingering
process of death from cancer which ended when he
asked his doctor to kill him? Jones (very like some of the
other biographers I've been considering) writes an "exemplary and heroic" death-scene, "a triumph of Freud's
belief in the reality principle," a picture of "a man facing

his fate without wish or illusion." Jones compares Freud's final gesture to Hamlet: "It said as plainly as possible, 'The rest is silence.'" (So the biographer is Horatio.) Gay makes no reference to Hamlet, but still places the emphasis on Freud's keeping control of his life, dying in his own fashion. Phillips comments: "For both Jones and Gay, the death, Freud's death, must say something about the life; must prove that the life was discernibly of a piece and that the death, therefore, was of a piece with the life. . . . Freud had unified himself." But the whole basis of Freudian analysis, and part of Freud's dislike of biography, was precisely that a life does not lend itself in this way to "straightforward intelligibility." Thus the biographers, while making Freud the hero of the deathbed, are also betraying Freud's own desire for self-fashioning. "Freud's heroic image of self-definition, of self-fashioning, is the notion that we want to die in our own way. The subject of a biography," Phillips concludes, appearing to concur with Freud at last, "always dies in the biographer's own way."[31]

In conclusion: biographical readings of their subject's end in which a gesture, a last word, or a final act are given value and significance, or in which the subject's work is invoked at the moment of death, sustain the old tradition of the deathbed scene that concludes the meaning of the life; but this may be quite incongruous for our post-Freudian, post-Beckettian times. Yet it is still very unusual for death in biography to occur as random, disorderly, without meaning, without relation to the life lived, and without conclusiveness. How to "treat" the death seemed to me one of the most difficult challenges in writing a biography of Virginia Woolf, whose death invites interpretation and mythologising. In her life, she was shadowed by death from childhood onwards. She persistently found ways of turning her grief for her lost dead, and her preoccupation with death, into fiction. But if the novel as "elegy" was one of her main inventions, she also wanted to sabotage the traditional presentation of deaths in fiction. This is how she kills off Mrs. Ramsay, in brackets, in *To the Lighthouse*:

> [Mr Ramsay stumbling along a passage stretched his arms out one dark morning, but, Mrs Ramsay having died rather suddenly the night before, he stretched his arms out. They remained empty.][32]

After the strong emotions which have gathered around Mrs. Ramsay in the first part of the book, the abrupt parenthesis is shocking. Nothing could be further from the prayers and weeping and solemn family gatherings of the traditional Victorian deathbed. Virginia Woolf goes out of her way in her fictions to avoid the melodramatic, necrophiliac lamentations which filled the darkened rooms of Hyde Park Gate after her mother's death. Though almost all her novels are dominated by a death, in almost all the death is not written in. Rachel, the young heroine of *The Voyage Out*, whose mother died when she was eleven, can barely say what she feels ("I am lonely," she began. "I want—").[33] She misremembers and can hardly mention her mother, who exists in the book as a gap or a silence. When Virginia Woolf does return to the death of the Victorian mother, in *The Years*, where at the start of the novel the Pargiter children are wearily waiting for it to happen, she writes a brilliantly alienated and unfeeling deathbed scene, which makes a cruel satire on the Victorian genre. These fictional death-scenes parallel her desire for biographies not to be like respectful obituaries or monuments.

So, faced with her death, which itself refused ceremony, attendance, or observation, the biographer encounters an acute problem of treatment. The causes of her death seem apparent. She had a history of suicidal breakdowns. War was placing her under great stress, with her houses in London bombed, air raids overhead and the imminent expectation of invasion. She and Leonard knew they were on Hitler's blacklist, and, like many of their friends, had made suicide plans. She felt extremely isolated living in the country. She was depressed on finishing her novel, *Between the Acts*, and convinced that it was worthless. She was making a distressing return to her childhood in her autobiography. She was, as at earlier moments of danger, finding it almost impossible to eat or sleep. She was obsessed by her own thoughts, her inner voices. All these are well-known factors. None of them, though, can ultimately explain the horrible and obscure moment of her suicide in the River Ouse on 28 March 1941, over sixty years ago.

But explanation is exactly what is wanted for such a death, and the explanations and making of myths began the moment the death was known. An accidental feature, the coroner's misreading of the suicide note at the inquest, contributed to the myth-making. What Virginia Woolf had said in one of her notes to Leonard was: "I feel certain that I am going mad again: I feel we can't go through another of those terrible times." What was read out in court, and reported in the papers, was: "I feel I am going mad. I cannot go through these terrible times."

Whereupon the wife of the Bishop of Lincoln wrote an outraged letter to the *Sunday Times*, commenting on the coroner's remark that Mrs. Woolf must have felt "the general beastliness of things more than most people." This, said the Bishop's wife, "belittles those who are carrying on unselfishly for the sake of others." And Leonard Woolf had to write letters to the papers explaining that this was not what Virginia had said.[34]

So the story of the feeble authoress giving up on the war effort began to be built into the posthumous myths of Virginia Woolf. That image of a nervous aesthetic creature, too fragile for her own good, was also being processed in the weeks after her death, by the (mostly male) writers who were paying their tributes to her, culminating in the special issue of *Horizon* in May 1941. When *Between the Acts* was published in July, the respectful reviews which greeted it persisted with the image of a thin-blooded, exquisitely imaginative writer, described by one reviewer as "a war casualty."[35] Since then, debate has continued over the death: on how much Leonard Woolf can be held responsible;[36] on how far back into childhood the causes of her death can be traced, and on whether her suicide was an act of insanity, or (as I read it) a rational act of courage. And now the death has been simplified, or Ophelia-ised, by the film of *The Hours*,[37] as the romantic immersion of a young woman with a very long nose in beautiful still waters, with music playing.

My view, when I wrote my biography, was that Virginia Woolf's suicide should not be made to fit a theory; and that all the information and all the interpretations should be written, or rewritten, as accurately as possible. But what I didn't want to do, or didn't feel I could do, was to write an account of her death which gave the impression that there was nothing mysterious and nothing obscure about that act. I could describe, as far as I knew it, how she ended it all, but I couldn't entirely—and nor can anyone—say why.

Notes

Introduction

1. Quotation from *The Quarterly Review*, 1856, copied by Gaskell into her manuscript of *The Life of Charlotte Bronte* (1857), quoted by Jenny Uglow, *Elizabeth Gaskell: A Habit of Stories*, Faber, 1993, p. 406.

2. Henry James, "James Russell Lowell," *Atlantic Monthly*, February 1892; quoted in Leon Edel, *The Life of Henry James*, Vol. II, pp. 28–29, and in David Ellis, *Literary Lives*, Edinburgh University Press, 2000, p. 124.

3. Samuel Johnson, *The Rambler*, No. 60, 13 October 1750, in James Clifford, Ed., *Biography as an Art: Selected Criticism, 1560–1960*, Oxford University Press, 1962, p. 42.

4. Virginia Woolf, "The Art of Biography" (1939), in *The Crowded Dance of Modern Life*, Penguin, 1993, p. 149.

5. John Dryden, "The Life of Plutarch," prefixed to *Plutarch's Lives, Translated from the Greek by Several Hands* (1683), in John Dryden, *Of Dramatic Poesy and other critical essays*, Everyman, Vol. II, 1962, p. 9.

Chapter 1. Shelley's Heart and Pepys's Lobsters

1. Ian Donaldson, "Biographical Uncertainty," *Dictionary of National Biography* Seminar, Oxford, January 2003.

2. Julian Barnes, *Flaubert's Parrot*, Cape, 1984, p. 38.

3. Hermione Lee, *Willa Cather: A Life Saved Up*, Virago, 1989, 1997, p. 330.

4. Charlotte Yonge, "Sir Thomas More's Daughter," in *A Book of Golden Deeds* (1864), Partridge, 1932, p. 176.

5. See, for variant versions, F. B. Pinion, *Thomas Hardy: His Life and Friends*, Macmillan, 1992, and Molly Lefebure, *Thomas Hardy's World*, Carlton, 1997.

6. Michael Paterniti, *Driving Mr Albert: A Trip Across America With Einstein's Brain*, Little, Brown, 2000.

7. Joseph Hone, *W. B. Yeats, 1865–1939*, Macmillan, 1942, pp. 477–9, R. F. Foster, *W. B. Yeats: A Life*, Vol. II, *The Arch-Poet*, Oxford University Press, 2003, pp. 728–29.

8. Richard Holmes, "Introduction," *Shelley: The Pursuit*, Weidenfeld & Nicolson, 1974; *Footsteps: Adventures of a Romantic Biographer*, Hodder & Stoughton, 1985, pp. 152–53. "Death and Destiny," on Shelley's afterlives, was first published in the *Guardian*, 24 January 2004, pp. 4–6, and delivered as a lecture at the National Portrait Gallery in the series "Interrupted Lives," on 29 January 2004. Holmes chaired an early version of my talk on "Shelley's Heart" at the conference on "Biographical Knowledge," University of Cambridge, Centre for Research in the Arts, Social Sciences and Humanities, 31 March 2003.

9. Holmes, *Shelley: The Pursuit*, pp. x–xi.

10. Ibid., p. 732; Ian Hamilton, *Keepers of the Flame*, Hutchinson, 1992, p. 131, Timothy Webb, *Shelley: A Voice Not Understood*, Manchester University Press, 1977, pp. 14–15.

11. Roger Smith et al., *The Shelley Legend*, Scribner's, 1945, p. 305.

12. Holmes, *Shelley: The Pursuit*, p. 353; William St Clair, "The Biographer as Archaeologist," in *Mapping Lives: The Uses of Biography*, ed. Peter France and William St Clair, Oxford University Press, 2002, p. 232.

13. Andrew Bennett, "Shelley's Ghosts," *Romantic Poets and the Culture of Posterity*, Cambridge University Press, 1999, p. 171.

14. Holmes, *Shelley: The Pursuit*, p. 730; William St Clair, *Trelawny: The Incurable Romancer*, John Murray, 1977, p. 217, David Crane, *Lord Byron's Jackal: A Life of Edward John Trelawny*, 1998, p. 48.

15. Edward Trelawny, *Recollections of the Last Days of Shelley & Byron*, Edward Moxon, 1858, chap. 12. 1858 version also in T. J. Hogg, *The Life of Shelley*, Vol. II, Dent, 1933.

16. Crane, *Lord Byron's Jackal*, p. 50.

17. See Webb, *Shelley*, p. 13; William St Clair, *Trelawny*, and Leslie A. Marchand, "Trelawny on the Death of Shelley," *Keats-Shelley Memorial Bulletin* 4 (1952): 9–34; Richard Holmes, "Death and Destiny," *Guardian*, 24 January 2004, p. 4.

18. *The Letters of Edward James Trelawny*, ed. H. Buxton Forman, Oxford University Press, 1910, p. 12; Marchand, "Trelawny on the Death of Shelley," p. 21; Trelawny, *Records of Shelley, Byron and the Author*, Basil Montagu Pickering, 1878, "Appendix," Vol. II, p. 241.

19. Leigh Hunt, *Autobiography*, 1850; ed. J. E. Morpurgo, Cresset Press, 1948, pp. 326–27, 331.

20. H. Buxton Forman, quoted by H. J. Massingham in *The Friend of Shelley: A Memoir of Edward James Trelawny*, Cobden-Sanderson, 1936, p. 174.

21. Edward Dowden, *The Life of Percy Bysshe Shelley*, 2 Vols, Kegan Paul, Trench & Co, 1886, pp. 576–79.

22. John Gisborne, "Shelley's Heart: A Memorandum by John Gisborne," in *Shelley and Mary*, 1882, Vol. III, pp. 867–68, and quoted in *Maria Gisborne and Edward Williams: Shelley's Friends, Their Journals and Letters*, ed. Frederick L. Jones, University of Oklahoma Press, 1951, p. 88.

23. "The Real Truth about Shelley's Heart," *My Magazine*, 29, 285, November 1933, pp. 939–43. F. L. Jones, ed., *The Letters of Mary Shelley*, University of Oklahoma Press, 1944, p. 187.

24. Miranda Seymour, *Mary Shelley*, John Murray, 2000, p. 306.

25. Holmes, "Death and Destiny," p. 4.

26. Mary Shelley to Maria Gisborne, 15 August and 27 August 1822, in *The Letters of Mary Shelley*, ed. Betty T. Bennett, Johns Hopkins University Press, 1980, pp. 253, 254.

27. *The Journals of Mary Shelley*, ed. Paula Feldman and Diana Scott-Kilvert, Clarendon Press, 1987, p. 444: 11 November 1822.

28. Crane, *Lord Byron's Jackal*, p. 57.

29. Holmes, *Shelley: The Pursuit*, pp. 658, 730.

30. Holmes, "Death and Destiny," p. 4.

31. Marcel Schwob, "Introduction," *Vies Imaginaires*, trans. Iain White, *The King in the Golden Mask and Other Writings*, Carcanet, 1982, p. 115. I am grateful to Ann Jefferson for telling me about Schwob.

32. Claire Tomalin, *Samuel Pepys: The Unequalled Self*, Viking, 2002, pp. 62, 83.

33. Ibid., p. 74.

34. Ibid., p. 306.

35. Ibid., p. 158; *The Diary of Samuel Pepys*, ed. R. Latham and W. Matthews, Viking, 1970–1983, Volume IV, p. 306: 13 September 1663.

36. Tomalin, *Samuel Pepys*, p. 164; Pepys, *Diary*, Vol. VIII, p. 303: 29 June 1667.

37. Tomalin, *Samuel Pepys*, pp. 261, 186; Pepys, *Diary*, Vol. VII, p. 164: 13 June 1666.

Chapter 2. Virginia Woolf's Nose

1. Conference on "Writing the Lives of Writers," Senate House, London, Centre for English Studies, London, 1–3 June 1995; proceedings published as *Writing the Lives of Writers*, ed. Warwick Gould and Thomas F. Staley, Macmillan, 1998.

2. Ted Hughes, in the *Independent*, 20 April 1989, quoted by Jacqueline Rose in *The Haunting of Sylvia Plath*, Virago, p. 67.

3. See, for a drily ironic version of such battles, Ian Hamilton, *Keepers of the Flame*, Hutchinson, 1992.

4. Holograph, Department of Manuscripts, British Library, reproduced in Hermione Lee, *Virginia Woolf*, Chatto & Windus, 1996, pp. 756, 759–60. The other note to Leonard Woolf is reprinted in *The Letters of Virginia Woolf*, ed. Nigel Nicolson and Joanne Trautmann, The Hogarth Press, 1975–1980, Vol. VI, Appendix A, opposite p. 489.

5. Elaine Showalter, "Introduction," *Mrs Dalloway*, 1925; Penguin, 1992, p. xxi.

6. "The Cinema," in *The Crowded Dance of Modern Life*, Penguin, 1993, p. 56.

7. *Mrs Dalloway*, Penguin, 1992, p. 23.

8. *The Diary of Virginia Woolf*, ed. Anne Olivier Bell and Andrew McNeillie, The Hogarth Press, 1977–1984, Vol. II, p. 263: 30 August 1923.

9. Ibid., p. 207: 14 October 1922.

10. *Mrs Dalloway*, p. 10.

11. Showalter, "Introduction," *Mrs Dalloway*, p. xxxvi, citing Woolf's introduction to the Modern Library edition of 1928.

12. Some argue that it's set on 13 June 1923, some on 20 June; David Bradshaw, in his notes to the Oxford World's Classics *Mrs Dalloway* (2000), pp. 182–83, argues for an "imaginary" Wednesday in June.

13. *Diary*, Vol. II, p. 283: 9 January 1924.

14. Michael Wood, review of *The Hours*, in the *New York Times Book Review*, 22 November 1998, p. 6.

15. Michael Cunningham, *The Hours*, 1998; Fourth Estate, 1999, p. 211.

16. Ibid., pp. 117, 33, 114, 153.

17. Ibid., p. 83.

18. Ibid., p. 8.

19. *Mrs Dalloway*, p. 10; Cunningham, *The Hours*, p. 8.

20. Wood, review of *The Hours*; Seymour Chatman, "*The Hours* as Second-Degree Narrative," forthcoming in *A Companion to Narrative Theory*, ed. James Phelan and Peter J. Rabinowitz, Blackwell, 2005. Quoted by permission of the author.

21. This point was made by Mary Desjardins in a panel discussion of *The Hours* at the Virginia Woolf Conference, Smith College, 6 June 2003.

22. Sean O'Connell, review of *The Hours*, Filmcritic.com, 2003.

23. Aidan Elliot, "Our Finest Hour," *Oxford Student*, 6 February 2003, report on Hermione Lee's interview with Stephen Daldry at the Phoenix Cinema, Oxford, www.oxfordstudent.com/2003-0206/culture/1.

24. Cunningham, *The Hours*, p. 151.

25. Mark Doty, *London Review of Books*, 14 November 2002, p. 8. Quoted by permission of the author.

26. Philip Hensher, *Daily Telegraph*, 24 January 2003.

27. Ed Gonzalez, *Slant magazine*, 2003; Hermione Lee, interview with Daldry.

28. Angela Wintle, "Decrying Woolf," *The Times*, 29 January 2003, p. 7; Virginia Nicholson to Hermione Lee, 11 February 2003. Quoted by permission of the author.

29. Roberta Rubenstein, "Outlook," *Washington Post*, 26 January 2003, p. 3.

30. Maria Alvarez, "Woolf at Our Door," www.theage.com.au/articles/2003/01/29/1043804404038.html.

31. Woolf's nose has been a bone of contention since well before *The Hours*. Brenda Silver, in *Virginia Woolf Icon*, an account of all the images, representations, and versions of Virginia Woolf, writes on how the

long aristocratic Stephen nose encouraged those critics who wanted to attack her as an upper-class snob (Chicago, 1999, pp. 139, 141).

32. Patricia Cohen, "The Nose Was the Final Straw," *New York Times*, 15 February 2003, pp. A19–21; Michael Cunningham, email to Hermione Lee, 19 February 2003. Quoted by permission of the author.

33. David Hare, "Introduction," *The Hours*, Miramax Books, 2002; Daniel Mendelsohn, "Not Afraid of Virginia Woolf", *New York Review of Books*, 13 March 2003; Panel discussion on *The Hours*, with Brenda Silver (Chair), Michèle Barrett, Daniel Mendelsohn, Leslie Hankins, Mary Desjardins, Virginia Woolf Conference, Smith College, 6 June 2003. Quoted by permission of the participants, and with thanks to Brenda Silver, Daniel Mendelsohn, and Michèle Barrett.

34. *Orlando* (1928), Penguin, 1993, p. 213; *To the Lighthouse* (1927), Penguin, 1992, p. 202.

Chapter 3. Jane Austen Faints

1. *Persuasion*, chaps. 17, 21.

2. "Caustic": Margaret Kirkham, *Jane Austen, Feminism and Fiction*, The Athlone Press, 1983, p. 59; "touched up": B. C. Southam, ed, *Jane Austen: The Critical Heritage*, Routledge & Kegan Paul, Vol. II, p. 4; Marilyn Butler, "Simplicity," *London Review of Books*, 5 March 1998, p. 3.

3. See Bruce Stovel, "Further Reading," in *The Cambridge Companion to Jane Austen*, ed. Edward Copeland and Juliet McMaster, Cambridge University Press, 1997, pp. 227–43; Deirdre Le Faye, *Jane Austen: A Family Record*, British Library, 1989, 2nd ed., Cambridge University Press, 2004; Kathryn Sutherland, "Introduction," *James Edward Austen-Knight: A Memoir of Jane Austen, and Other Family Recollections*, Oxford University Press, 2002, p. xxv.

4. Claire Tomalin, *Jane Austen: A Life*, Viking, 1997, p. 122; Deirdre Le Faye, *Jane Austen's Letters*, Oxford University Press, 1995, pp. xiv–xviii; Carol Houlihan Flynn, "The Letters," in *The Cambridge Companion to Jane Austen*, pp. 100–114; Sutherland, "Introduction," p. xxx.

5. Le Faye, *Jane Austen*, 2004, pp. 143–44.

6. Constance Pilgrim, *Dear Jane: A Biographical Study*, Pentland Press, 1971, described by John Wiltshire, in *Recreating Jane Austen*,

Cambridge University Press, 2001, p. 13, as "a wonderful, ridiculous book"; Joan Rees, *Jane Austen: Woman and Writer*, Robert Hale, 1976, p. 88; John Halperin, *The Life of Jane Austen*, Johns Hopkins University Press and Harvester, 1984, p. 133. On "pathological" readings, see Claudia L. Johnson, *Jane Austen: Women, Politics and the Novel*, University of Chicago Press, 1988, p. 120. On Cassandra's invention, see David Nokes, *Jane Austen: A Life*, Fourth Estate, 1997, p. 243; "mistily romantic": Tomalin, *Jane Austen: A Life*, 1997, p. 179.

7. "A very domestic woman": Butler, "Simplicity," 1998, p. 3; "veneration": Carol Shields, *Jane Austen*, Weidenfeld & Nicolson, 2001, p. 146; Henry Austen, "Biographical Notice," 1818, reprinted in the Penguin edition of *Northanger Abbey*, 1972, p. 31; "ladylike image": Jan Fergus, "The Professional Woman Writer," in *The Cambridge Companion to Jane Austen*, p. 12.

8. James Austen-Leigh, *A Memoir of Jane Austen*, 1870, reprinted in the Penguin edition of *Persuasion*, 1994, pp. 331, 387, 389. On its characteristics and reception, see Margaret Kirkham, *Jane Austen: Feminism and Fiction*, pp. 58–59; "a comfortable, approachable figure": B. C. Southam, ed., *Jane Austen: The Critical Heritage*, Vol. II, pp. 2–5. "We might and we did": Clara Tuite, *Romantic Austen: Sexual Politics and the Literary Canon*, Cambridge University Press, 2002, p. 25.

9. Deidre Lynch, *Janeites: Austen's Disciples and Devotees*, Princeton University Press, 2000, p. 7.

10. Butler, "Simplicity," p. 3.

11. "Regulated Hatred: An Aspect of the work of Jane Austen," *Scrutiny* 8 (1940): 346–62, in Ian Watt, ed, *Jane Austen: A Collection of Critical Essays*, Prentice Hall, 1963, p. 169; Marvin Mudrick, *Jane Austen: Irony as Defence and Discovery*, Princeton University Press, 1952.

12. Marilyn Butler, *Jane Austen and the War of Ideas*, Clarendon Press, 1975; against her view, see Alistair Duckworth, *The Improvement of the Estate: A Study of Jane Austen's Novels*, Johns Hopkins University Press (1971), 1994, p. xxv, and Jon Mee, "Jane Austen's Treacherous Ivory," in *The Post-Colonial Jane Austen*, ed. You-Me Park and Rajeswari Sunderrajan, Routledge, 2000, p. 76.

13. Nigel Nicolson, *The World of Jane Austen*, Weidenfeld & Nicolson, 1991, cited in John Wiltshire, *Recreating Jane Austen*, p. 37.

Susan Watkins, *Jane Austen in Style*, Thames & Hudson, 1996, p. 7, first published 1990 as *Jane Austen's Town and Country Style*. "Golden age": Mary Evans, *Jane Austen and the State*, Tavistock publications, 1987, p. x; "harmonious refuge": Deidre Lynch, "At Home with Jane Austen," in *Cultural Institutions of the Novel*, ed. Deidre Lynch and William B. Warner, Duke University Press, 1996, p. 172; "angelic dismay": Ivor Morris, *Jane Austen and the Interplay of Character*. The Athlone Press, 1987, p. 163.

14. For good summaries of the different critical positions on Austen, see Rajeswari Sunderajan, ("gendered public-private ascription"), "Austen in the World: Postcolonial Mappings," in *The Post-Colonial Jane Austen*, pp. 3–25; Deidre Lynch on the Austen Industry in "At Home with Jane Austen," *Cultural Institutions of the Novel*, pp. 159–92; Clara Tuite on the "canonical constructions" of Austen in *Romantic Austen: Sexual Politics and the Literary Canon*, Cambridge University Press, 2002; Deidre Lynch, *Janeites: Austen's Disciples and Devotees*, Princeton University Press, 2000; and Claudia L. Johnson, "Austen Cults and Cultures," in *The Cambridge Companion to Jane Austen*, pp. 211–26. For Austen as "deeply involved," see Alistair Duckworth, *The Improvement of the Estate*, p. xxv.

15. On Chapman's editions, see Claudia L. Johnson, "Austen Cults and Cultures," in *The Cambridge Companion to Jane Austen*, pp. 217–19, and B. C. Southam, ed, *Jane Austen: The Critical Heritage*, Vol. II, pp. 99–100. "fleas": Roger Sales, *Jane Austen and Representations of Regency England*, Routledge, 1994, p. 10. Critical of capitalism: Mary Evans, *Jane Austen and the State*, p. 1. Jane and Cassandra: Terry Castle, "Sister-Sister" [headlined by the *London Review of Books* editor, "Was Jane Austen Gay?"], *London Review of Books*, 3 August 1995, reprinted in *Boss Ladies, Watch Out!*, Routledge, 2002. Edward Said, "Jane Austen and Empire" (1989), in *Culture and Imperialism*, Vintage, 1994. "Green core": Clara Tuite, "Domestic retrenchment and imperial expansion: the property plots of *Mansfield Park*," in *The Post-Colonial Jane Austen*, p. 112.

16. Carolyn Heilbrun, *Writing a Woman's Life* (1988) Ballantine Books, 1989, pp. 30–31.

17. Jane Austen to Cassandra Austen, 27–28 October 1798, *Jane Austen's Letters: New Edition*, ed. Deirdre Le Faye, Oxford University Press, 1995, p. 17.

18. Deirdre Le Faye, *Jane Austen: A Family Record*, p. 128.

19. Sutherland, "Introduction," p. xl. Wiltshire, *Recreating Jane Austen*, p. 17.

20. On the Leavisite construction of "Augustan Austen," Johnsonian and satirical, writing a comedy of civilised life, see Clara Tuite, *Romantic Austen*, pp. 2–5.

21. John Mullan, *Sentiment and Sensibility: The Language of Feeling in the Eighteenth Century*, Clarendon Press, Oxford, 1988, p. 217. Emma Austen-Leigh, *Jane Austen and Bath*, 1939; republished with an introduction by David Gilson, Routledge, 1995, p. 13; A. C. Bradley, "Jane Austen" (1911), in *A Miscellany*, Macmillan, 1929, p. 71.

22. John Wiltshire, *Jane Austen and the Body*, Cambridge University Press, 1992, pp. 8, 12, 140.

23. "Timid": Jon Mee, in *The Post-Colonial Jane Austen*, p. 87. "Green nook": Deidre Lynch, "At Home with Jane Austen," in *Cultural Institutions of the Novel*, p. 189. "Bath": Clara Tuite, *Romantic Austen*, p. 163. "Enjoying herself": Margaret Kirkham, *Jane Austen, Feminism and Fiction*, 1983; rev. ed. The Athlone Press, 1997, pp. 61–63.

24. Bruce Stovel, "Further Reading," in *The Cambridge Companion to Jane Austen*, p. 229. John Halperin, *The Life of Jane Austen*, 1984, pp. 123–24, 132. Park Honan, *Jane Austen: Her Life*, Weidenfeld & Nicolson, 1987, pp. 155–56.

25. Claire Tomalin, *Jane Austen: A Life*, Viking, 1997, pp. 75, 261, 142, 205, 170–75.

26. Carol Shields, *Jane Austen*, pp. 150–51, 73–83.

27. David Nokes, *Jane Austen: A Life*, 1997, pp. 220–22, 254, 350–51, 410, 491.

28. Wiltshire, *Recreating Jane Austen*, p. 35.

29. *Mansfield Park*, chap. 22.

Chapter 4. How to End It All

1. Philippe Ariès, *Western Attitudes towards Death*, Marion Boyars, 1976, pp. 11, 55, 37, 68.

2. Philippe Ariès, *The Hour of Our Death*, trans. Helen Weaver, Allen Lane, 1981, p. 569.

3. See Douglas Davies, *Death, Ritual and Belief*, Cassell, 1997; Claire Gittings, *Death, Burial and the Individual in Early Modern*

England, 1984; Peter Jupp and Claire Gittings, eds., *Death in England*, Manchester, 1999; Pat Jalland, *Death in the Victorian Family*, Oxford University Press, 1996; R. Houlbrooke, ed, *Death, Ritual and Bereavement*, Routledge, 1989; John Wolffe, *Great Deaths*, Oxford University Press, 2000.

4. Jalland, *Death in the Victorian Family*, p. 8; Wolffe, *Great Deaths*, p. 61; Davies, *Death Ritual and Belief*, p. 7.

5. David Hume, *Dialogues concerning Natural Religion*, ed. Norman Kemp Smith, Nelson, 1981, pp. 243–48; James Boswell, "An Account of My Last Interview with David Hume, Esq.," from *The Private Papers of James Boswell*, ed. G. Scott and F. Pottle, Vol. XII (1931), pp. 227–32; Bruce Redford, *Designing the Life of Johnson*, Oxford University Press, 2002, pp. 143–4. I am grateful to Tony Nuttall for alerting me to Hume's deathbed words.

6. Wolffe, *Great Deaths*, pp. 158, 178.

7. Robert Southey, *Life of Nelson*, 2 Vols, John Murray, 1813; Vol. I, 1832, pp. 290, 296.

8. Jalland, *Death in the Victorian Family*, p. 33; see pp. 33–37 on nineteenth-century last words.

9. *The Art of Dying* (1930), ed. Francis Birrell and F. L. Lucas, The Hogarth Press, 1930; *The Oxford Book of Death*, ed. D. J. Enright (1983) 1987.

10. Enright, *Oxford Book of Death*, p. 314.

11. Janet Malcolm, *Reading Chekhov*, Granta, 2003, pp. 63–73.

12. Frank Kermode, *The Sense of an Ending*, Oxford University Press (1966) 1968, p. 8.

13. Edmund White, *Genet*, Chatto & Windus, 1993, p. 729.

14. Julian Barnes, *Flaubert's Parrot*, Cape, 1984, p. 181.

15. Lytton Strachey, *Queen Victoria* (1921); Penguin, 1971, p. 246.

16. Bruce Redford, *Designing the Life of Johnson*, Oxford University Press, 2002, pp. 9–10.

17. John Halperin, *The Life of Jane Austen*, Harvester, 1984, p. 352.

18. D. J. Taylor, *Orwell: The Life*, Chatto & Windus, 2003, p. 424.

19. Peter Ackroyd, *Dickens*, Sinclair-Stevenson, 1990, Chap. 21.

20. See David Amigoni, *Victorian Biography: Intellectuals and the Ordering of Discourse*, Harvester, 1993.

21. Ackroyd, *Dickens*, pp. xi–xii.

22. Juliet Barker, *The Brontës*, Weidenfeld & Nicolson, 1994, p. 576.

23. Victoria Glendinning, *Trollope*, Hutchinson, 1992.

24. Jenny Uglow, *Elizabeth Gaskell: A Habit of Stories*, Faber, 1993, p. 616.

25. André Maurois, *The Quest for Proust*, Cape, 1950, p. 332.

26. George Painter, *Marcel Proust*, Chatto & Windus, 1965, pp. 363, 364.

27. Samuel Beckett, *Proust*, John Calder, 1965, p. 17.

28. Jean-Yves Tadié, *Marcel Proust* (1996); Viking, trans. Euan Cameron, 2000.

29. Andrew Motion, *Philip Larkin*, Faber, 1993, p. 521.

30. Alan Bullock, *Hitler and Stalin: Parallel Lives*, HarperCollins, 1991, p. 1067; Peter Gay, *Freud: A Life for Our Time*, Dent, 1988, p. 651.

31. Adam Phillips, "The Death of Freud," in *Darwin's Worms*, Faber, 1999, pp. 67–111.

32. Virginia Woolf, *To the Lighthouse* (1927); Penguin, 1992, p. 140.

33. Virginia Woolf, *The Voyage Out* (1915); Oxford University Press, 2001, p. 62.

34. See Hermione Lee, *Virginia Woolf*, Chatto & Windus, 1996, chap. 40.

35. Malcolm Cowley, *New Republic*, 6 October 1941, in *Virginia Woolf: The Critical Heritage*, ed. Robin Majumdar and Allen McClaurin, Routledge, 1975, p. 449.

36. See Phyllis Grosskurth, *Times Literary Supplement*, 31 October 1980, pp. 1225–26, reviewing the last volume of Virginia Woolf's letters—("In the official search, how thoroughly was the river dragged?. . . . How could her body have been wedged in some underwater debris? It would surely have required some very heavy rocks to have held it down, until it was found three weeks later, floating like a decomposed Ophelia")—and Nigel Nicolson's response to these suggestions as "absurd" (*Times Literary Supplement*, 23 January 1981).

37. See my earlier chapter on "Virginia Woolf's Nose."

Index

··